The Knitting Stitch Bible

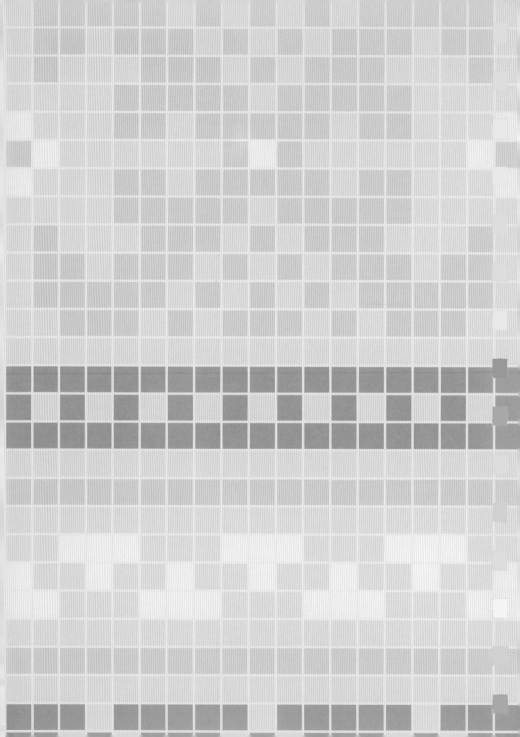

The Knitting Stitch Bible

Maria Parry-Jones

CHARTWELL
BOOKS, INC.

A QUARTO BOOK

This edition published in 2009 by
CHARTWELL BOOKS, INC.
A division of BOOK SALES, INC.
276 Fifth Avenue Suite 206
New York, New York 10001
USA

Reprinted 2009

ISBN-13: 978-0-7858-2551-7
ISBN-10: 0-7858-2551-7

QUAR.KSB

Acknowledgments
I would like to thank many people for their generosity in helping
compile and write this book, including my sister, Sharon, for her
administrative help, and my mother, Eira M Jones, as well as Gill
Barker and Marion Evans, all of whom helped knit swatches.
Without them this book may never have been completed. I
would also like to thank Hayley Phillips and James Partridge for
their technical help and advice. Finally, I would like to thank
Pauline Hornsby for her tireless checking of swatches and charts.
Maria Parry-Jones

Conceived, designed, and produced by
Quarto Publishing plc
The Old Brewery
6 Blundell Street
London N7 9BH

Printed in China
by SNP Leefung Printers Limited

The Knitting Stitch Bible

Contents

Introduction ————— 6

How to Use this Book ——— 8
Reading charts ————— 8

Hand Knitting Essentials—— 10
Yarns ————— 10
Reading a ball band————— 11
Needles ————— 12
Other equipment ———— 13

The Stitch Selector ———— 16

The Stitch Collection——— 32
Knit & purl ————— 32
Rib————— 65
Cable————— 89
Bobble————— 122
Lace————— 147
Fair Isle————— 181
Intarsia————— 213
Sequins & beads ————— 238

Chart Symbols————— 250
Abbreviations ————— 256

Introduction

This book has been designed to meet the needs of all knitters—from the absolute beginner to the more accomplished—who want to explore the craft of hand knitting in a creative and imaginative way. How you use the book will depend on the level of your skills as a knitter, but I hope that through its use, your skills will develop enormously.

My love of knitting began at the age of three when I was taught to knit by my aunt and, as my parents bred angora goats, I also took a keen interest in hand spinning and the various fibers available. My interest in knitwear continued to grow, eventually leading to a BSc (hons) in knitwear design, and I now work as a knitwear designer and consultant.

Knitting knowledge has traditionally been passed on directly from one generation to another. Before the dramatic change in family life over the past decades, there was usually a grandmother or aunt nearby to give assistance, and for a long time young people have tended to regard knitting as a pastime for old women. In recent years, a renewed interest in knitting has blossomed and many young knitters are now attracted to the craft by the designer influence and the modern yarns now available. Knitting is suddenly back in vogue, and designers have demonstrated that this versatile craft can be used for high fashion garments, found in designer boutiques and shopping malls.

This book contains a broad range of designs in seven different types of knitting, as well as a section on embellishments, which offers a sample of beaded or sequined swatches from each of the seven categories. Wherever possible, both swatches and charts have been reproduced at 100 percent, and the type of wool used has been provided so that the same effect can be achieved.

Charts have been used rather than patterns, as they are a better means of expressing the stitch techniques required for each stitch design. They are more concise and easy to follow than stitch-by-stitch instructions and, because they provide a visual element, are also easier to memorize. Learning to work from these charts is not a difficult task—just take it one step at a time.

Once you have grasped the knitting process and the way in which the graphs work, confidence will develop naturally. As with any task, faith in your own ability is the most important factor. Knitting is, after all, simply a series of loops, the structure, neatness, and design of which are totally in the hands of the knitter. Knitting can become a very enjoyable pastime, which, as well as being useful and highly creative, has an extraordinarily therapeutic value: it is very relaxing and helps to calm our modern-day lives.

Just remember, be creative, help others, and enjoy yourself.

Happy Knitting!
Maria Parry-Jones

How to Use this Book

The book has been divided into eight chapters, covering basic knit & purl, rib, cable, bobble, lace, Fair Isle, and intarsia designs, finishing with a section on embellishments. If you already know which pattern you want to use, the Stitch Selector (pages 16-31) will help you find it quickly, and also allows you to see the full range of patterns at a glance.

Swatches have been photographed and reproduced at 100 percent (or, where space does not permit this, as close to 100 percent as possible) to provide an accurate impression of the finished design.

Reading charts

Unlike patterns that consist of rows of abbreviations, charts are visual and pictorial, and are easily used by knitters of all ages and abilities. Futhermore, seeing the charted image of the construction in front of you enables you to add or subtract stitches and rows from the design and, once you have grasped the symbol indicating the stitch construction, it is easy to follow and adapt patterns.

- Each square on the chart represents a stitch, and each row a new row of stitches.

- Each chart is numbered on both sides, the right-hand side has odd numbers, and the left-hand side has even numbers.

- The numbers start at the bottom right-hand side, so you follow a chart by reading from right to left, bottom to top.

- The slightly thicker lines in the charts represent pattern repeats.

Chart A: Knit & purl

◉ Purl on right side, knit on wrong side (p1).

☐ Knit on right side and purl on wrong side (k1).

Chart A therefore reads:
1. p1, k1, p1, k1.
2. p1, k1, p1, k1.
3. k1, p1, k1, p1.
4. k1, p1, k1, p1.

Chart B: Lace

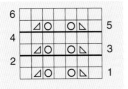

⊙ Yarn forward and over needle to
form stitch (yf)

◪ Knit two together (k2tog)

◪ Slip one, knit one, pass slip stitch
over (skpo)

Graph B therefore reads:
1. k1, skpo, yf, k1, yf,
   k2tog, k1.
2. p to end
Repeat these two rows to form
the pattern.

Charts C and D: Cable

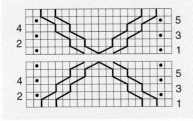

▭▭▭ On RS rows, slip 2 stitches
onto cable needle and hold
at front of work, k2, then k2
from cable needle.

On WS rows, slip 2 stitches
onto cable needle and hold at
front of work, p2, then p2
from cable needle.

▭▭▭ On RS rows, slip 2 stitches
onto cable needle and hold at
back of work, k2, then k2
from cable needle.

On WS rows, slip 2 stitches
onto cable needle and hold at
back of work, p2, then p2
from cable needle.

Chart E: Intarsia

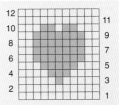

Intarsia charts are easy to follow
because each stitch is represented by
its color. Intarsia knitting is usually
knitted in stockinette, so every right
side row is knitted and every wrong
side row is purled.

A full list of chart symbols is
provided on p 250 and a full list
of abbreviations is on p 256.

9

Hand Knitting Essentials

Yarn

There is a wonderful range of new yarns on the market today. Not only are there new yarns in natural fibers, but also many interesting synthetic yarns, and their qualities have been improved enormously. There is also a greater variety of fibers available in terms of weight, finish, and thickness, from the finest thread-like yarn to huge chunkies, and many unusual and novelty yarns with bizarre finishes.

Synthetic fibers have improved over the years, and synthetics are sometimes added to natural fibers to reduce the price. Be aware that garments made from 100 percent synthetic yarns tend to loose their shape easily.

When interchanging yarns, check the tension square on the ball band, this will tell you the amount of rows and stitches within a 4-inch (10cm) square. Also check the yardage of the ball of yarn. The yardage can vary extensively due to fiber compositions. Finally, the most important aspect you need to check is the dye lot number. Different dye lots vary subtly in shading, which may not be apparent when you are comparing two balls of yarn.

Yardage

Yarn	Stitches & Rows	Needle size	Length & weight per ball
4-ply	28 sts by 36–38 rows	2–4	186 yds (170m), 3½ oz (50 g)
Light-weight	23 sts by 32 rows	2–4	125 yds (115m), 1¾ oz (50g)
DK (double-knit)	21–24 sts by 29–33 rows	5–6	191 yds (175m), 1¾ oz (50g)
Medium-weight	20 sts by 28 rows	6–7	93 yds (85m), 1¾ oz (50g)
Aran-weight	16–18 sts by 23–26 rows	8 or 9	98 yds (90m), 1¾ oz (50g)
Chunky	13–15 sts by 19–22 rows	10	109 yds (100m), 3½ oz (100g)

Reading a Ballband

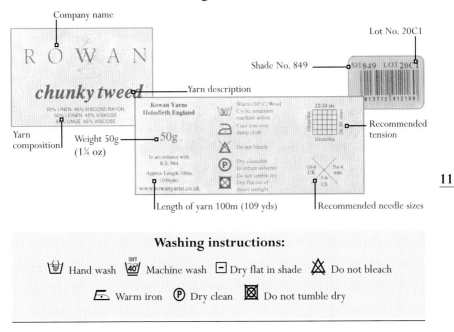

Company name

Lot No. 20C1

Shade No. 849

Yarn description

Recommended tension

Yarn composition

Weight 50g (1¾ oz)

Length of yarn 100m (109 yds)

Recommended needle sizes

Washing instructions:

Hand wash   Machine wash   Dry flat in shade   Do not bleach

Warm iron   Dry clean   Do not tumble dry

Needles

Before you begin to knit a project, a variety of hand knitting equipment is required. The most essential item required is, of course, a pair of knitting needles.

Needles are made in various lengths and thicknesses (see opposite), and are also made of different materials: metal, plastic, and bamboo. I recommend using bamboo needles because they do not make the clicking noise, they are much smoother, and are lighter to use. If you suffer at all from arthritis, bamboo needles are warmer to touch and, being made of organic materials, are preferable.

Sizing

Old English	US	Metric
13	1	2.25mm
12	2	2.75mm
11	2–3	3mm
10	3–4	3.25mm
9	5	3.75mm
8	6	4mm
7	7	4.5mm
6	8	5mm
5	9	
4	10	5.5mm
3	10.5	6mm
2	10.5	
1	11	6.5mm
0	11	7mm
00	13	
000	15	7.5mm
00000	19	
		8mm
		9mm
		10mm
		15mm

Other Equipment

Other equipment includes cable needles, stitch holder, crochet hooks, scissors, a tape measure, yarn sewing needles, pins, latch tool, safety pins and a row counter.

- **Cable needles**
  These are used for holding stitches when knitting cables. These needles can be straight or have a slight bend in them.

- **Yarn bobbins**
  These are used in multicolor knitting. Each colored yarn is wound around a separate bobbin.

- **Scissors**
  Choose small sharp scissors for cutting yarn and thread.

- **Tape measure**
  Use a tape measure to work out the width and height of the stitches in relation to the recommended tension listed on the yarn's ball band.

- **Pins and sewing needles**
  Pins are used for holding knitted material in place prior to steaming or sewing. Knitters' sewing needles, which usually have a blunt end, are used for sewing together pieces of knitted fabric, and for concealing yarn ends in the finished piece.

14

Stitch holders
A stitch holder works much like a safety pin, and holds in reserve stitches that need to be worked later.

Row counters
Placed at the end of one of the knitting needles, each time a row is completed, one of the digits is turned.

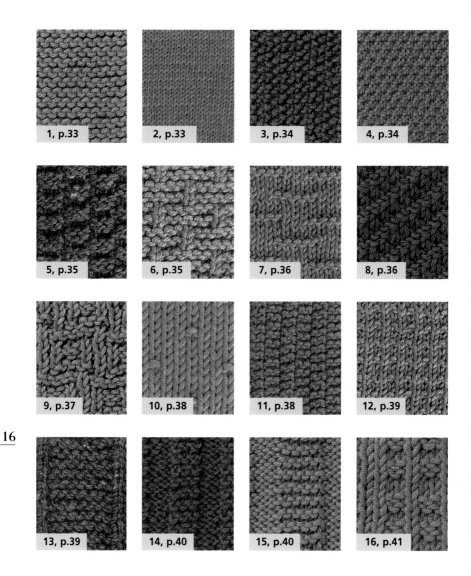

1, p.33

2, p.33

3, p.34

4, p.34

5, p.35

6, p.35

7, p.36

8, p.36

9, p.37

10, p.38

11, p.38

12, p.39

13, p.39

14, p.40

15, p.40

16, p.41

16

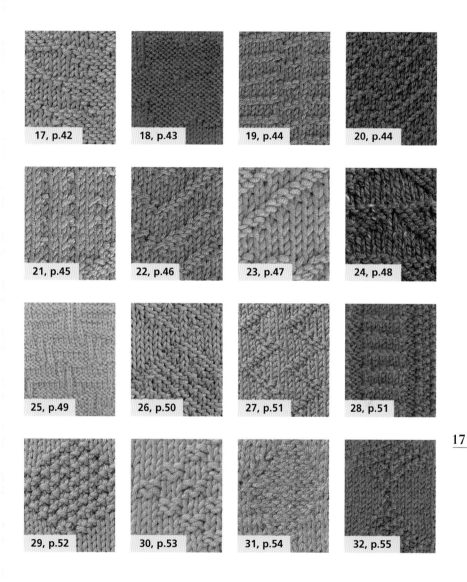

17

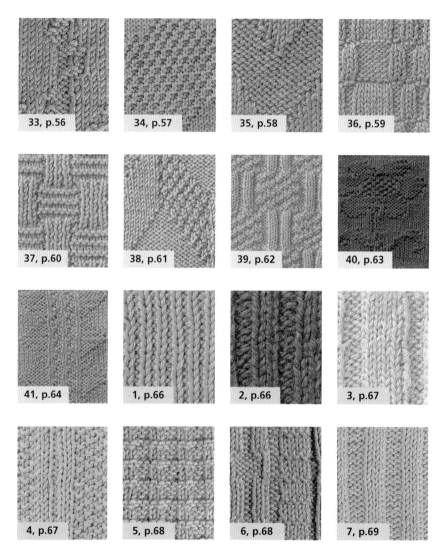

33, p.56

34, p.57

35, p.58

36, p.59

37, p.60

38, p.61

39, p.62

40, p.63

41, p.64

1, p.66

2, p.66

3, p.67

18

4, p.67

5, p.68

6, p.68

7, p.69

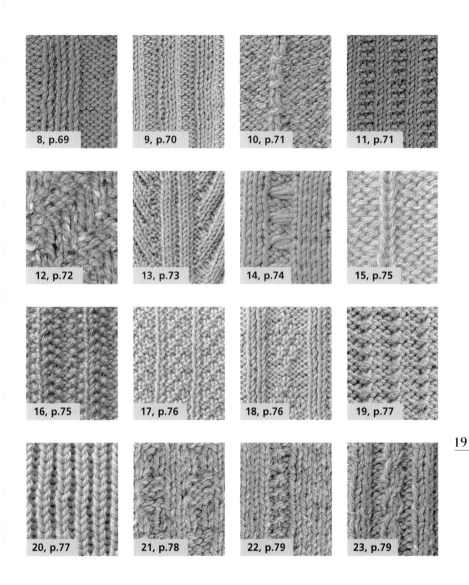

8, p.69
9, p.70
10, p.71
11, p.71
12, p.72
13, p.73
14, p.74
15, p.75
16, p.75
17, p.76
18, p.76
19, p.77
20, p.77
21, p.78
22, p.79
23, p.79

19

The Stitch Selector

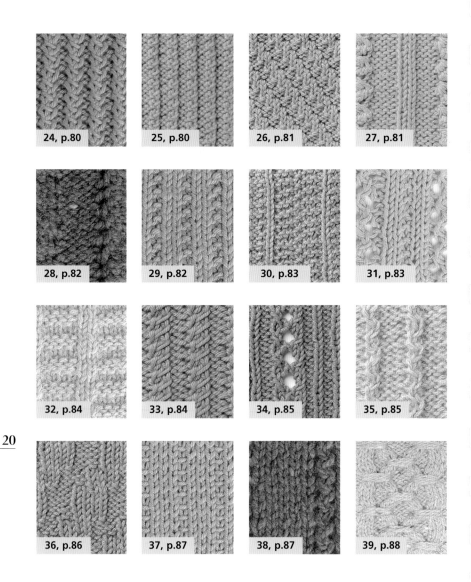

24, p.80

25, p.80

26, p.81

27, p.81

28, p.82

29, p.82

30, p.83

31, p.83

32, p.84

33, p.84

34, p.85

35, p.85

36, p.86

37, p.87

38, p.87

39, p.88

20

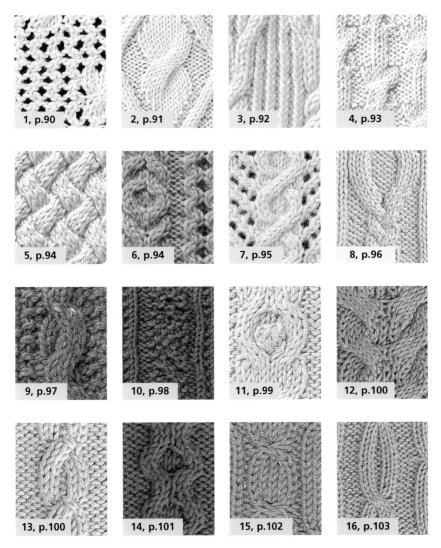

1, p.90
2, p.91
3, p.92
4, p.93
5, p.94
6, p.94
7, p.95
8, p.96
9, p.97
10, p.98
11, p.99
12, p.100
13, p.100
14, p.101
15, p.102
16, p.103

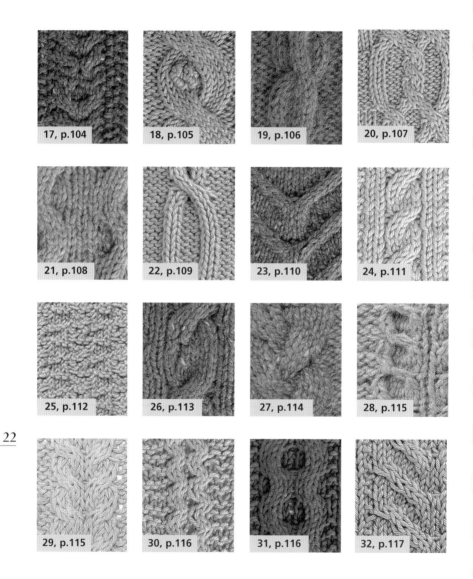

17, p.104

18, p.105

19, p.106

20, p.107

21, p.108

22, p.109

23, p.110

24, p.111

25, p.112

26, p.113

27, p.114

28, p.115

29, p.115

30, p.116

31, p.116

32, p.117

22

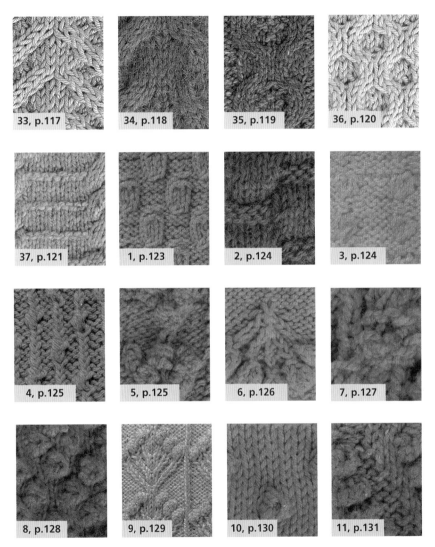

33, p.117

34, p.118

35, p.119

36, p.120

37, p.121

1, p.123

2, p.124

3, p.124

4, p.125

5, p.125

6, p.126

7, p.127

8, p.128

9, p.129

10, p.130

11, p.131

23

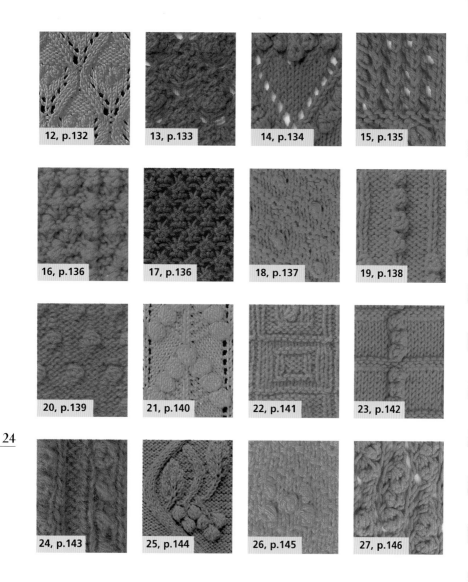

12, p.132

13, p.133

14, p.134

15, p.135

16, p.136

17, p.136

18, p.137

19, p.138

20, p.139

21, p.140

22, p.141

23, p.142

24, p.143

25, p.144

26, p.145

27, p.146

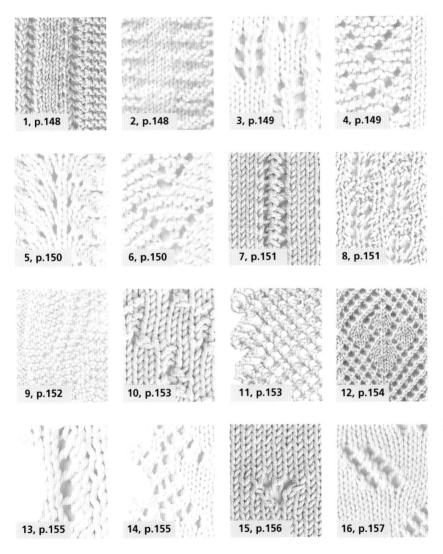

1, p.148

2, p.148

3, p.149

4, p.149

5, p.150

6, p.150

7, p.151

8, p.151

9, p.152

10, p.153

11, p.153

12, p.154

13, p.155

14, p.155

15, p.156

16, p.157

25

The Stitch Selector

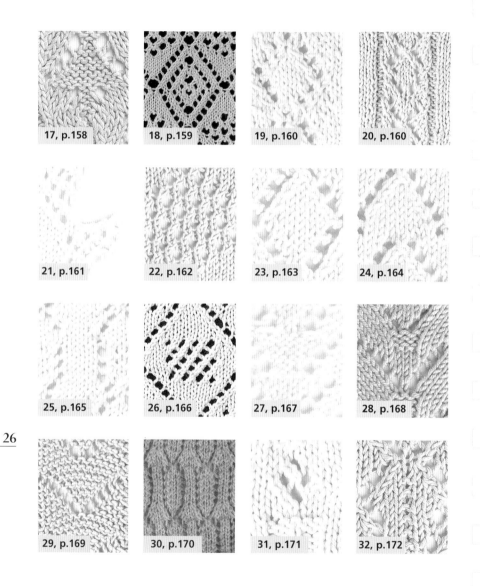

17, p.158

18, p.159

19, p.160

20, p.160

21, p.161

22, p.162

23, p.163

24, p.164

25, p.165

26, p.166

27, p.167

28, p.168

29, p.169

30, p.170

31, p.171

32, p.172

26

33, p.173

34, p.174

35, p.175

36, p.176

37, p.177

38, p.178

39, p.179

40, p.180

1, p.182

2, p.183

3, p.184

4, p.185

5, p.186

6, p.187

7, p.188

8, p.188

27

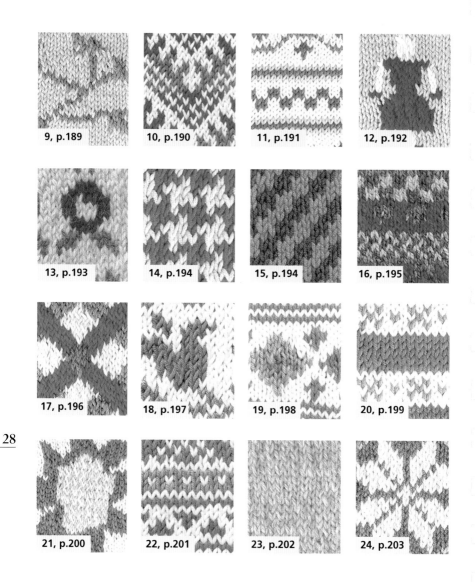

9, p.189

10, p.190

11, p.191

12, p.192

13, p.193

14, p.194

15, p.194

16, p.195

17, p.196

18, p.197

19, p.198

20, p.199

21, p.200

22, p.201

23, p.202

24, p.203

28

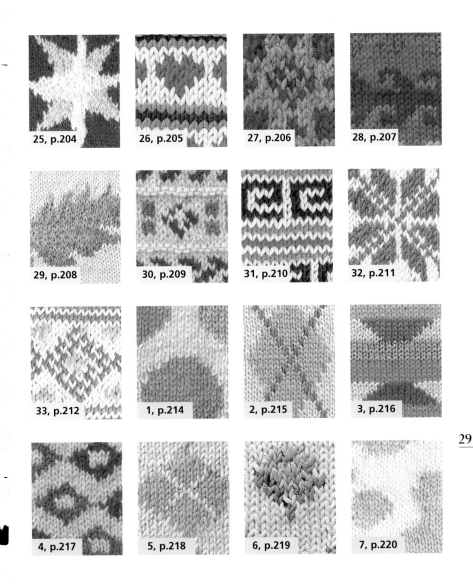

25, p.204

26, p.205

27, p.206

28, p.207

29, p.208

30, p.209

31, p.210

32, p.211

33, p.212

1, p.214

2, p.215

3, p.216

4, p.217

5, p.218

6, p.219

7, p.220

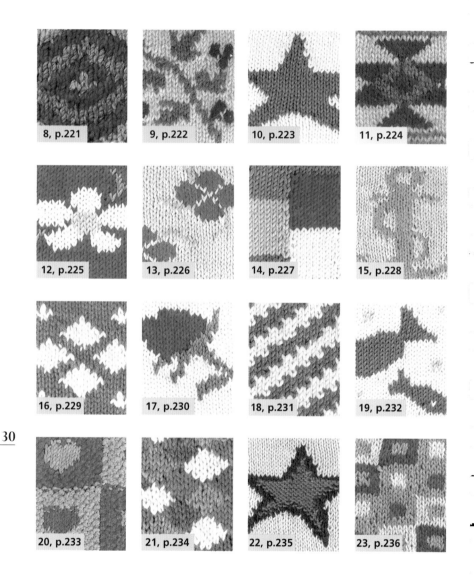

8, p.221

9, p.222

10, p.223

11, p.224

12, p.225

13, p.226

14, p.227

15, p.228

16, p.229

17, p.230

18, p.231

19, p.232

20, p.233

21, p.234

22, p.235

23, p.236

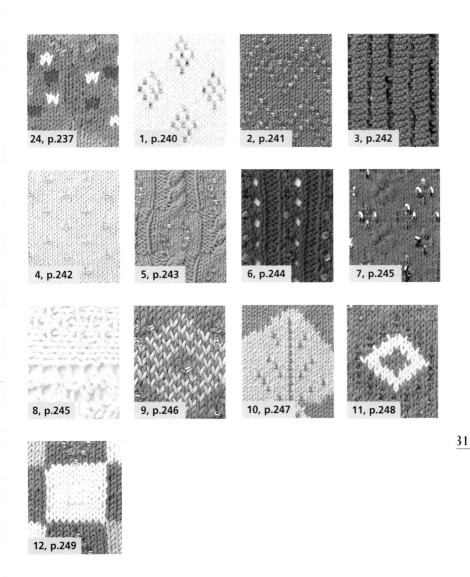

24, p.237

1, p.240

2, p.241

3, p.242

4, p.242

5, p.243

6, p.244

7, p.245

8, p.245

9, p.246

10, p.247

11, p.248

12, p.249

31

1

KNIT & PURL

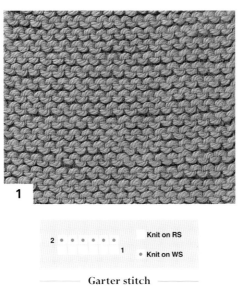

2	•	•	•	•	•	•	Knit on RS
						1	• Knit on WS

Garter stitch

Medium-weight cotton, multiple of 1 stitch

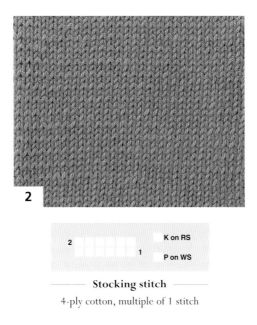

2							K on RS
						1	P on WS

Stocking stitch

4-ply cotton, multiple of 1 stitch

The Stitch Collection

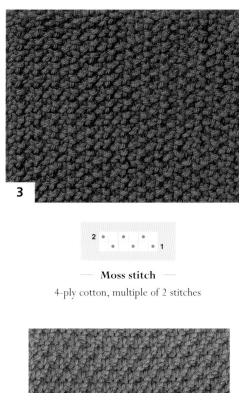

3

2 • • • •
• • • • 1

— **Moss stitch** —

4-ply cotton, multiple of 2 stitches

4

4 • • • •
• • • • 3
2 • • • •
• • • • 1

——— **Double moss stitch** ———

4-ply cotton, multiple of 2 stitches

The Stitch Collection

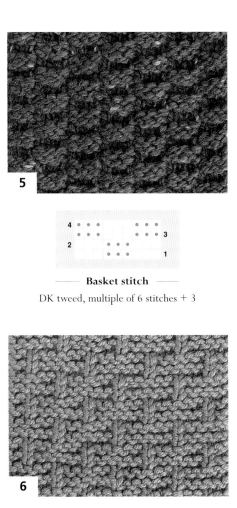

5

4 • • •   • • •
      • • •   • • • 3
2 •   • • •
          • • •   1

—— **Basket stitch** ——

DK tweed, multiple of 6 stitches + 3

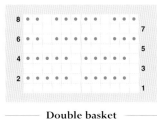

6

8 • •   • • • •   • • •
      • •   • • •   • • 7
6 • •   • • •   • • •
      • •   • • •   • • 5
4 • • •   • • • •   • • •
      • •   • • •   • • 3
2 • • • •   • • • •
      • • •   • • •   1

—— **Double basket** ——

DK wool cotton, multiple of 6 stitches

The Stitch Collection

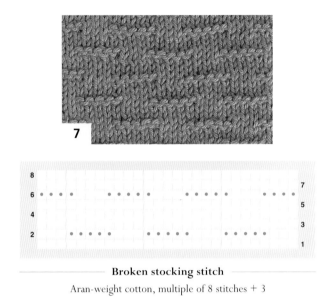

7

Broken stocking stitch
Aran-weight cotton, multiple of 8 stitches + 3

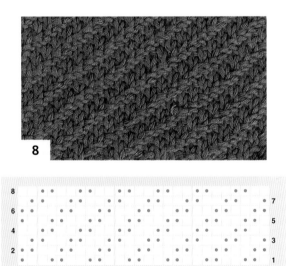

8

Diagonal structure
DK linen, multiple of 8 stitches + 2

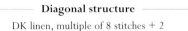

9

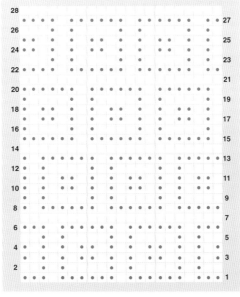

Structured squares

Light-weight cotton, multiple of 7 stitches

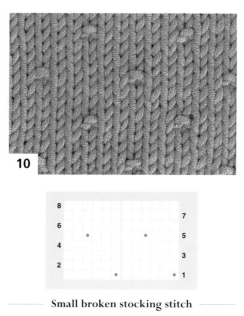

10

8						
6						7
		•		•		5
4						3
2						
			•		•	1

Small broken stocking stitch

Aran-weight cotton, multiple of 6 stitches

11

2		•	•		•	•	
	•	•		•	•	•	1

Knit & purl stitch

4-ply cotton, multiple of 4 stitches

The Stitch Collection

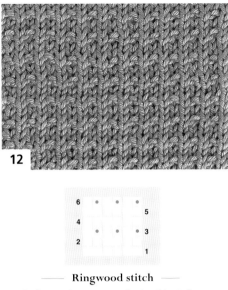

12

6	•	•	•	
				5
4				
	•	•	•	3
2				1

—— **Ringwood stitch** ——

Light-weight cotton, multiple of 2 stitches

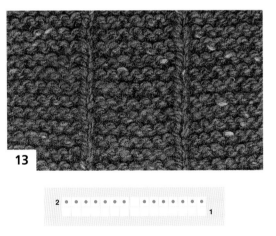

13

2	• • • • • • •	• • • • • • •	
			1

—— **Broken garter stitch** ——

DK tweed, multiple of 8 stitches + 7

The Stitch Collection

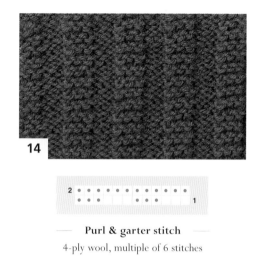

14

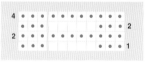

— **Purl & garter stitch** —

4-ply wool, multiple of 6 stitches

15

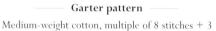

— **Garter pattern** —

Medium-weight cotton, multiple of 8 stitches + 3

The Stitch Collection

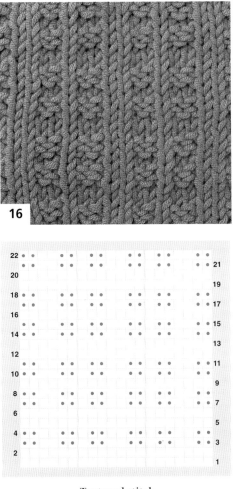

16

Textured stitch

Aran-weight cotton, multiple of 7 stitches + 6

The Stitch Collection

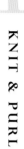

17

Knit & purl structure

Light-weight cotton, multiple of 10 stitches + 1

The Stitch Collection

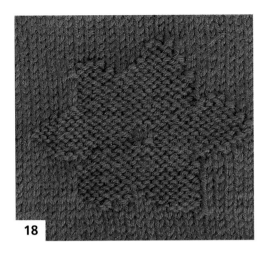

18

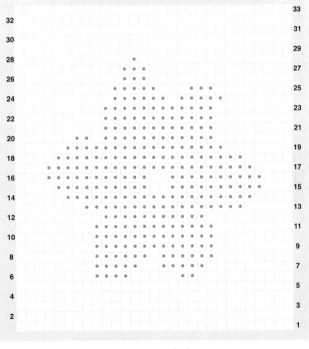

Structure stitch

4-ply wool, multiple of 29 stitches

The Stitch Collection

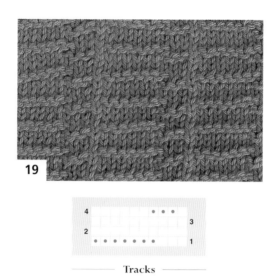

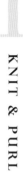

19

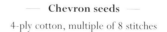

Tracks

4-ply cotton, multiple of 10 stitches

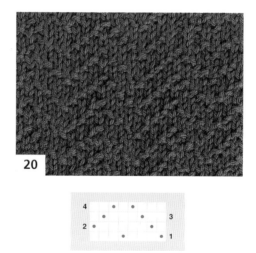

20

Chevron seeds

4-ply cotton, multiple of 8 stitches

44

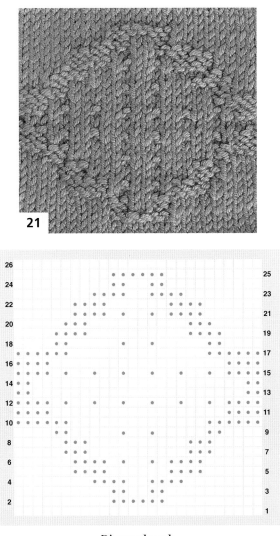

21

Diamond seeds

DK wool cotton, multiple of 26 stitches

The Stitch Collection

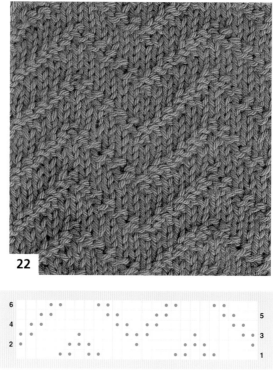

22

Delicate chevrons

4-ply cotton, multiple 12 stitches + 1

46

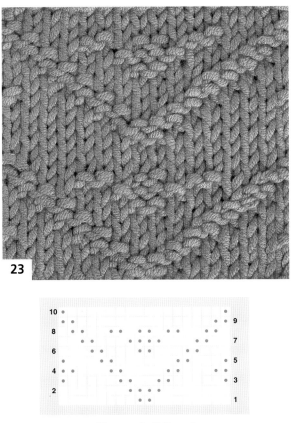

23

10																	

Chevron knit & purl

Aran-weight cotton, multiple of 18 stitches

The Stitch Collection

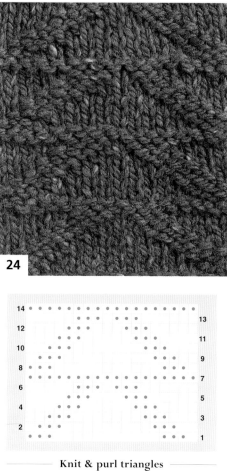

24

Knit & purl triangles

DK tweed, multiple of 18 stitches

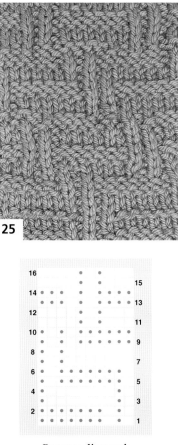

25

Reverse diagonals

Medium-weight cotton, multiple of 10 stitches

The Stitch Collection

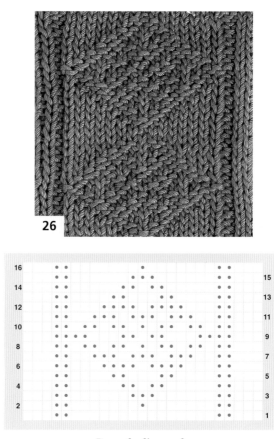

Brocade diamonds

Light-weight cotton, multiple of 25 stitches

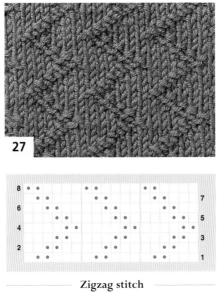

27

8 · ·   · ·   · ·
    ·   ·   · 7
6   · ·   · ·   · ·
     ·   ·   · 5
4   · ·   · ·   · ·
   ·   ·   · 3
2   · ·   · ·   · ·
   ·   · ·   · · 1

Zigzag stitch
DK wool cotton, multiple of 6 stitches

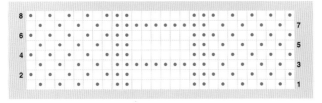

28

Ladder moss stitch & pleated purl
4-ply wool, multiple of 19 stitches + 9

The Stitch Collection

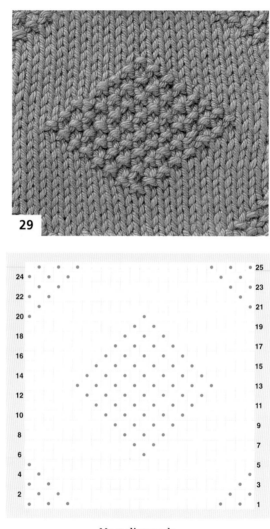

29

Moss diamonds

Medium-weight cotton, multiple of 24 stitches

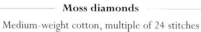

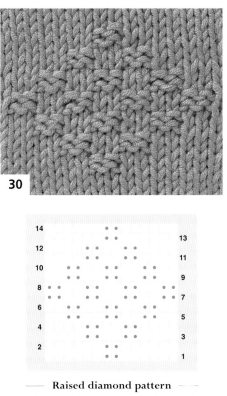

30

— **Raised diamond pattern** — —

Medium-weight cotton, motif of 14 stitches

The Stitch Collection

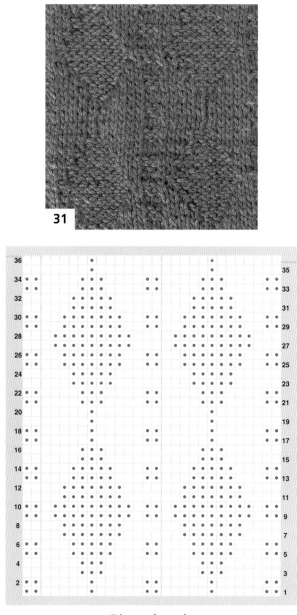

31

Diamond panels

4-ply cotton, multiple of 13 stitches + 2

The Stitch Collection

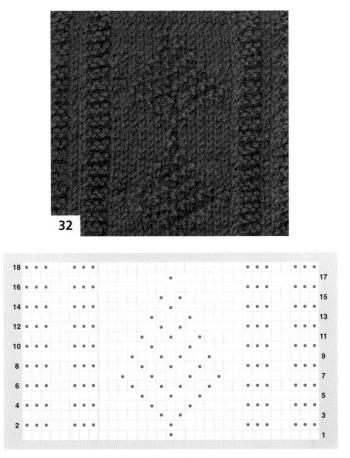

32

Tree of life

4-ply wool, multiple of 23 stitches + 8

The Stitch Collection

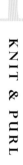

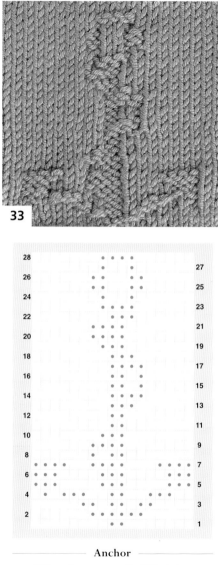

33

Anchor

DK wool cotton, motif of 17 stitches

The Stitch Collection

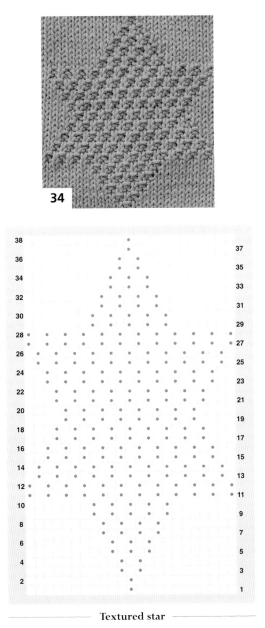

34

Textured star

Light-weight cotton, motif of 23 stitches

The Stitch Collection

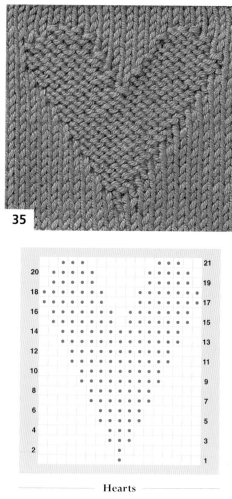

35

Hearts

DK wool cotton, motif of 17 stitches

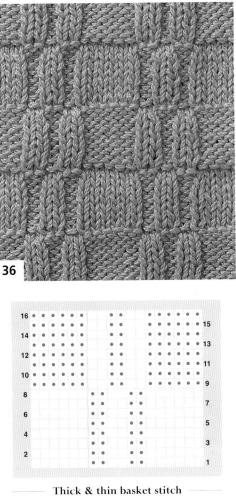

36

Thick & thin basket stitch

Light-weight cotton, multiple of 12 stitches + 6

The Stitch Collection

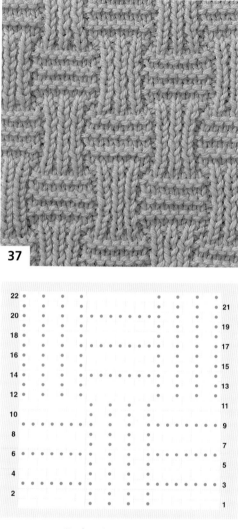

37

Basket & garter stitch

Medium-weight cotton, multiple of 14 stitches + 7

The Stitch Collection

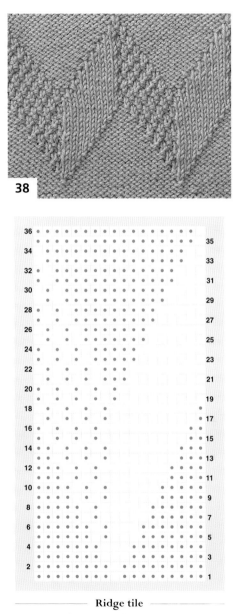

38

36
35
34
33
32
31
30
29
28
27
26
25
24
23
22
21
20
19
18
17
16
15
14
13
12
11
10
9
8
7
6
5
4
3
2
1

— **Ridge tile** —
DK linen, multiple of 18 stitches

The Stitch Collection

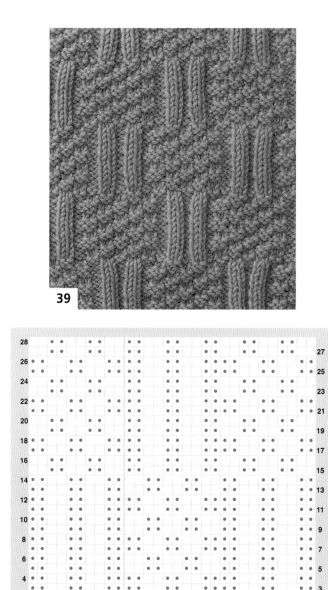

39

Textured moss and rib patchwork stitches

DK wool cotton, multiple of 20 stitches + 10

T h e   S t i t c h   C o l l e c t i o n

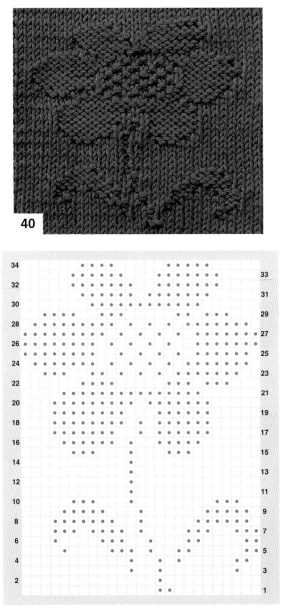

40

Embossed flower motif

Medium-weight cotton, motif of 25 stitches

T h e   S t i t c h   C o l l e c t i o n

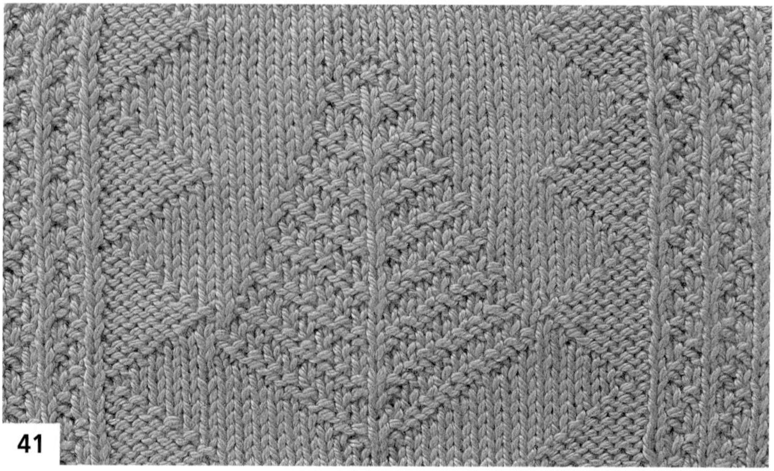

41

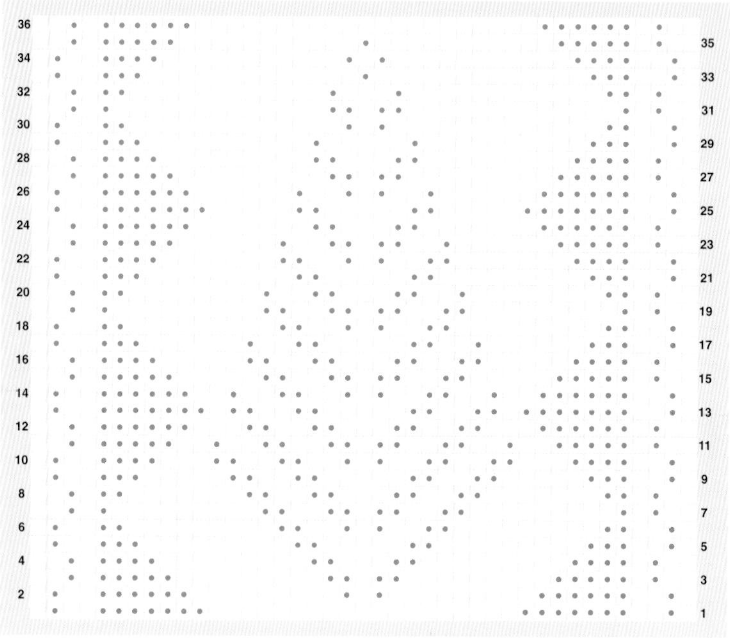

64

The tree of life with purl triangles

4-ply cotton, multiple of 40 stitches +1

2

RIB

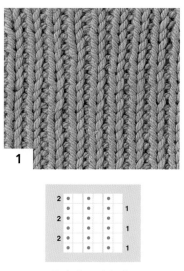

1

— **Knit 1 purl 1 rib** —

Medium-weight cotton, multiple of 2 stitches

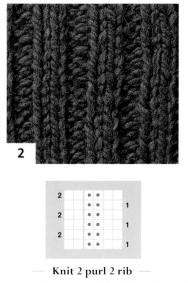

2

66

— **Knit 2 purl 2 rib** —

Aran-weight wool, multiple of 4 stitches + 2

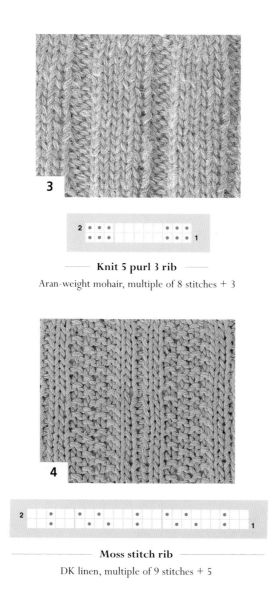

3

2	•	•	•						•	•	•	
	•	•	•					•	•	•		1

Knit 5 purl 3 rib
Aran-weight mohair, multiple of 8 stitches + 3

4

Moss stitch rib
DK linen, multiple of 9 stitches + 5

2

RIB

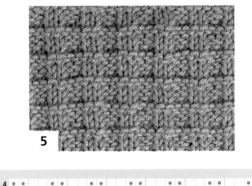

5

Ridge rib

4-ply cotton, multiple of 4 stitches + 2

6

68

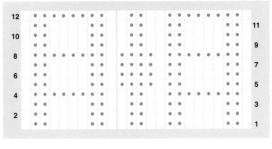

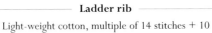

Ladder rib

Light-weight cotton, multiple of 14 stitches + 10

The Stitch Collection

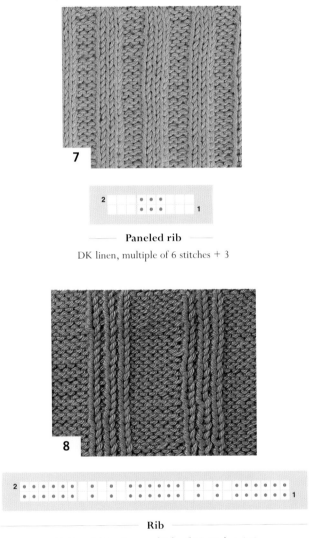

7

		•	•	•		
2		•	•	•		1

Paneled rib

DK linen, multiple of 6 stitches + 3

8

Rib

Light-weight cotton, multiple of 11 stitches + 6

The Stitch Collection

RIB

9

Treble track rib

4-ply cotton, multiple of 24 stitches + 3

The Stitch Collection

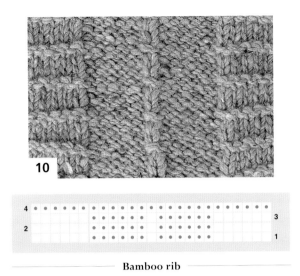

10

Bamboo rib

DK tweed, multiple of 19 stitches + 6

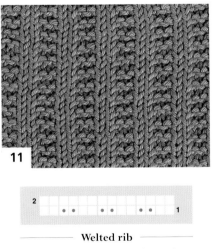

11

2

1

Welted rib

Light-weight cotton, multiple of 4 stitches + 2

The Stitch Collection

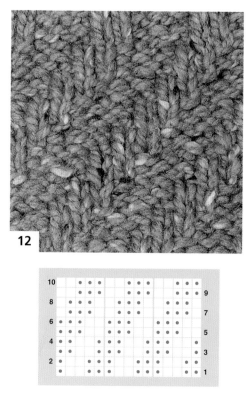

12

Diagonal rib

Chunky tweed, multiple of 5 stitches

72

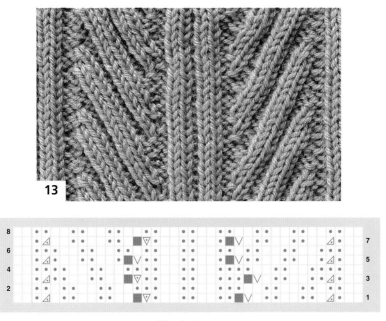

13

8															

Herringbone

DK tweed, multiple of 36 stitches + 2

The Stitch Collection

2

14

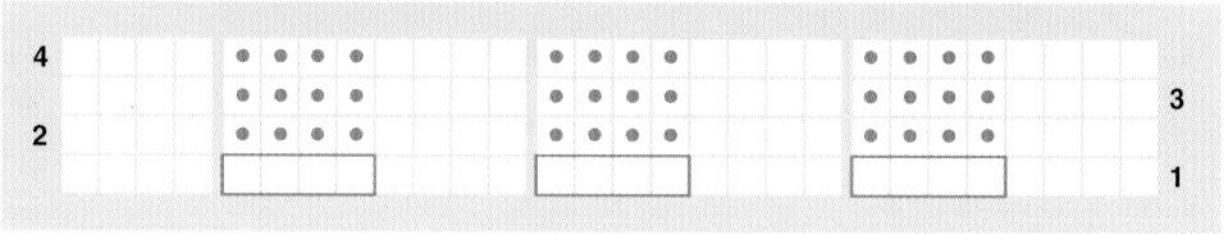

Chunky bamboo

Medium-weight cotton, multiple of 8 stitches + 4

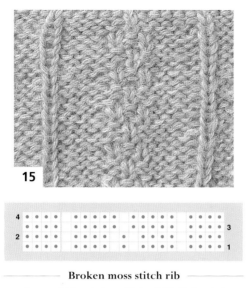

15

Broken moss stitch rib

Aran-weight mohair, multiple of 17 stitches + 4

16

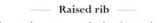

--- **Raised rib** ---

Light-weight cotton, multiple of 4 stitches + 3

The Stitch Collection

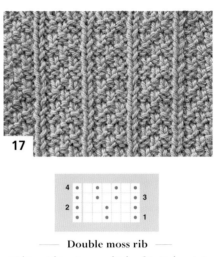

17

Double moss rib

Light-weight cotton, multiple of 6 stitches + 1

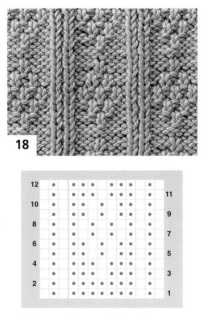

18

Double moss diamond in a rib structure

4-ply cotton, multiple of 10 stitches + 3

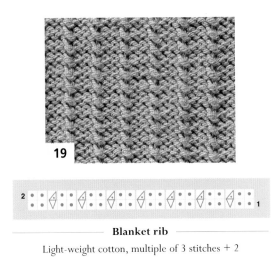

19

Blanket rib

Light-weight cotton, multiple of 3 stitches + 2

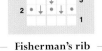

20

Fisherman's rib

Medium-weight wool, multiple of 2 stitches + 3

multiple of 2 rows + 1

The Stitch Collection

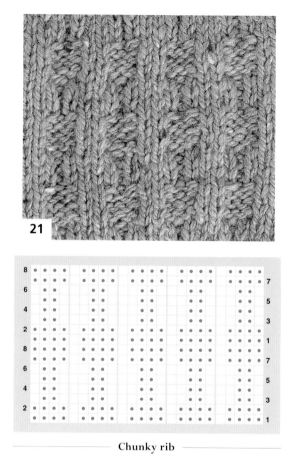

Chunky rib

DK tweed, multiple of 5 stitches + 4

The Stitch Collection

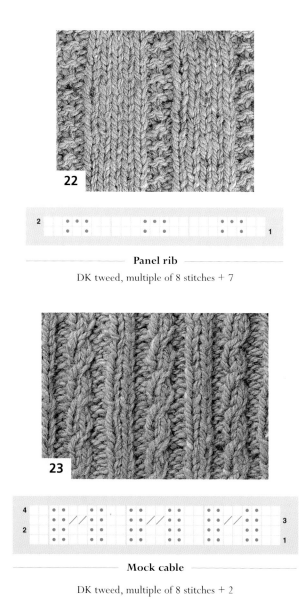

Panel rib

DK tweed, multiple of 8 stitches + 7

Mock cable

DK tweed, multiple of 8 stitches + 2

The Stitch Collection

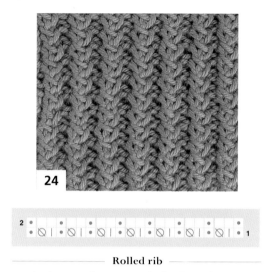

Rolled rib

Medium-weight cotton, multiple of 3 stitches + 1

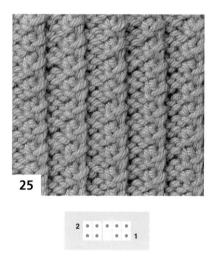

Rib columns

Light-weight cotton, multiple of 3 stitches + 2

The Stitch Collection

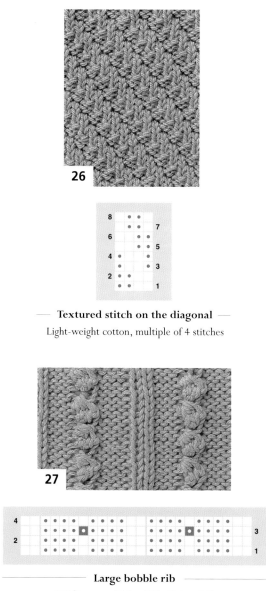

26

— Textured stitch on the diagonal —
Light-weight cotton, multiple of 4 stitches

27

— Large bobble rib —
DK linen, multiple of 11 stitches + 2

The Stitch Collection

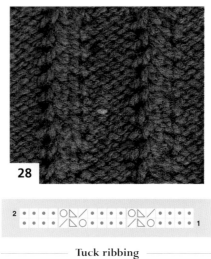

Tuck ribbing

Aran-weight wool, multiple of 7 stitches + 4

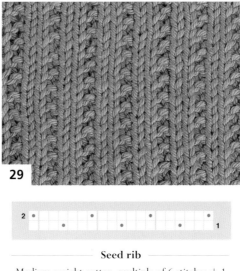

Seed rib

Medium-weight cotton, multiple of 6 stitches + 1

The Stitch Collection

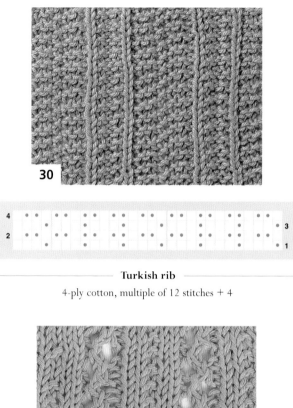

30

Turkish rib
4-ply cotton, multiple of 12 stitches + 4

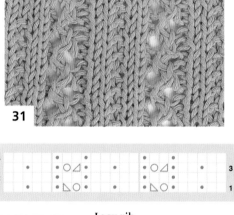

31

Lacy rib
DK linen, multiple of 9 stitches + 5

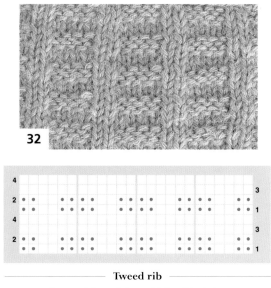

Tweed rib

Aran-weight mohair, multiple of 6 stitches

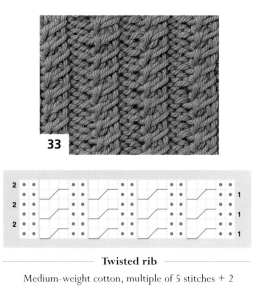

Twisted rib

Medium-weight cotton, multiple of 5 stitches + 2

The Stitch Collection

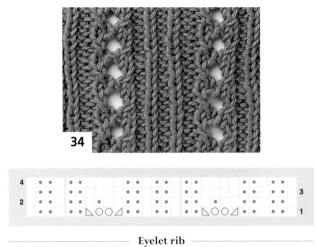

34

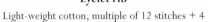

Eyelet rib

Light-weight cotton, multiple of 12 stitches + 4

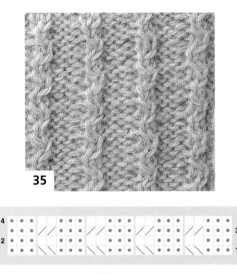

35

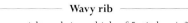

Wavy rib

Aran-weight mohair, multiple of 5 stitches + 3

The Stitch Collection

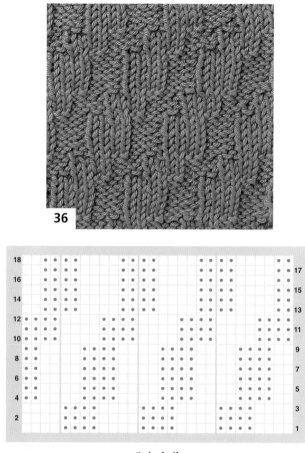

36

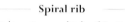

Spiral rib

Light-weight cotton, multiple of 8 stitches + 4

The Stitch Collection

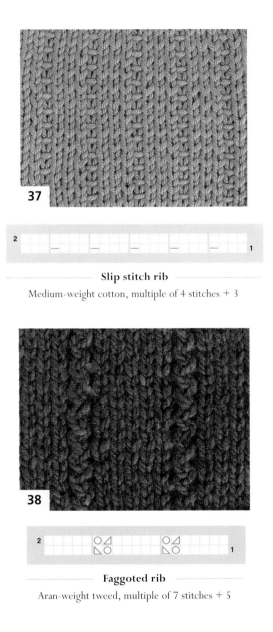

37

| | | — | | — | | — | | — | | — | | 1 |

2

Slip stitch rib

Medium-weight cotton, multiple of 4 stitches + 3

38

2

Faggoted rib

Aran-weight tweed, multiple of 7 stitches + 5

The Stitch Collection

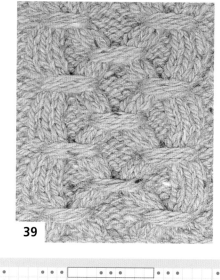

39

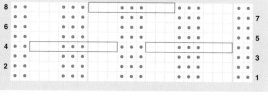

Smocked rib

DK tweed, multiple of 15 stitches + 10

CABLE

3

CABLE

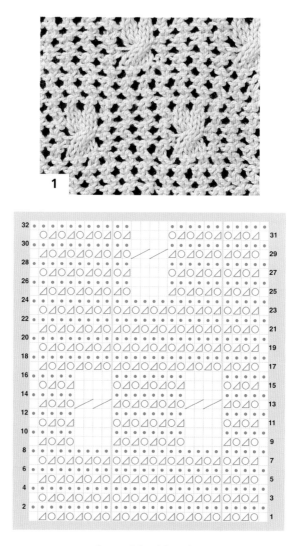

Lace with cable twist

DK linen, multiple of 12 stitches + 14

The Stitch Collection

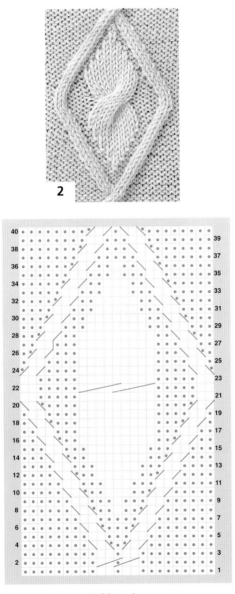

Cable twist
in a diamond

Medium-weight cotton, multiple of 23 stitches

The Stitch Collection

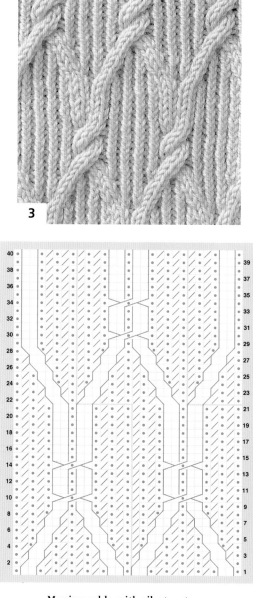

Moving cable with rib structure

Light-weight cotton, multiple of 14 stitches + 15

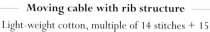

The Stitch Collection

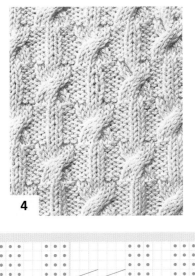

4

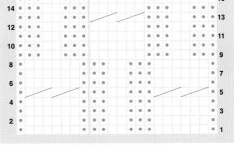

Rib & cable twist

4-ply cotton, multiple of 14 stitches + 8

The Stitch Collection

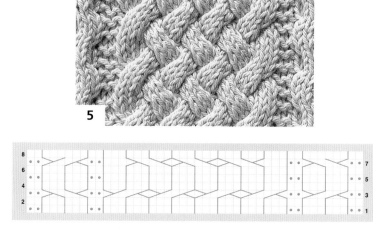

Plaited structure with snake cable

Light-weight cotton, panel of 44 stitches

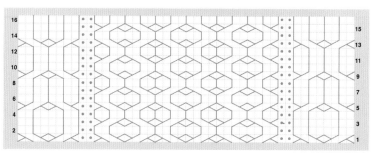

Honeycomb with oxo

DK tweed, panel of 44 stitches

The Stitch Collection

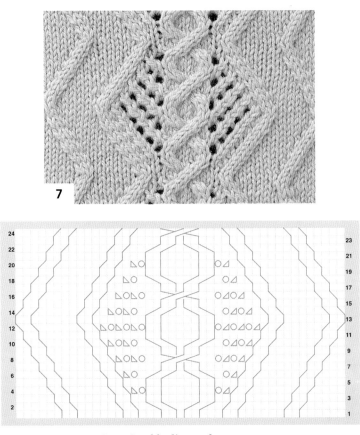

Lace & cable diamond structure

DK tweed, panel of 43 stitches

95

The Stitch Collection

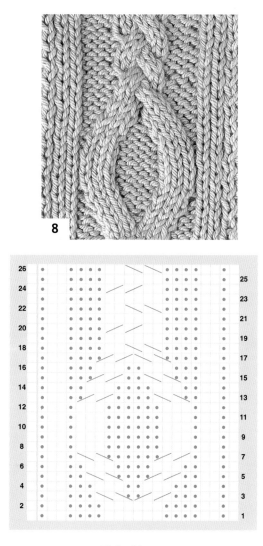

8

Plaited loops

Medium-weight cotton, multiple of 21 stitches + 1

The Stitch Collection

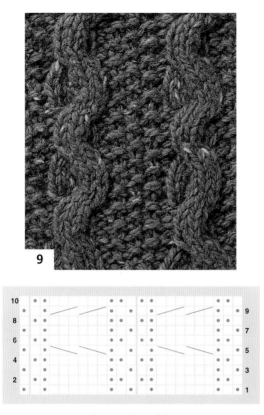

9

Serpentine cable
DK tweed, multiple of 11 stitches + 1

CABLE

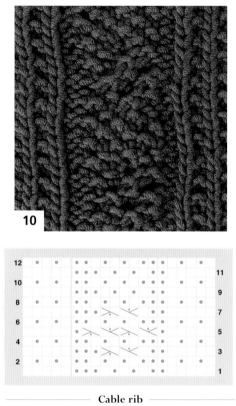

10

Cable rib
Aran-weight cotton, multiple of 15 stitches + 5

The Stitch Collection

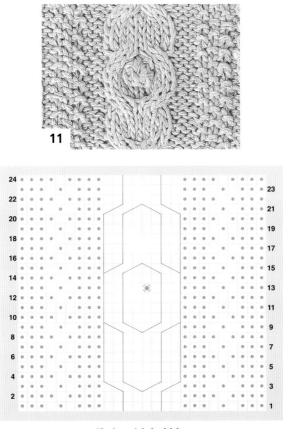

11

Chain with bobbles

DK linen, multiple of 17 stitches + 9

The Stitch Collection

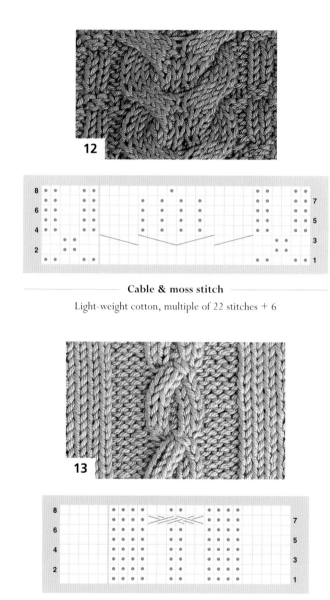

12

Cable & moss stitch

Light-weight cotton, multiple of 22 stitches + 6

13

Chain cable

Medium-weight cotton, multiple of 19 stitches + 5

The Stitch Collection

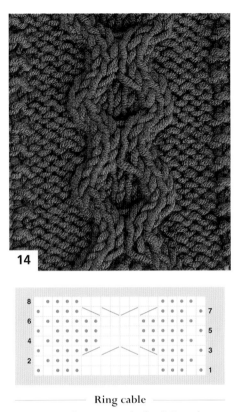

14

Ring cable

Aran-weight cotton, multiple of 18 stitches

The Stitch Collection

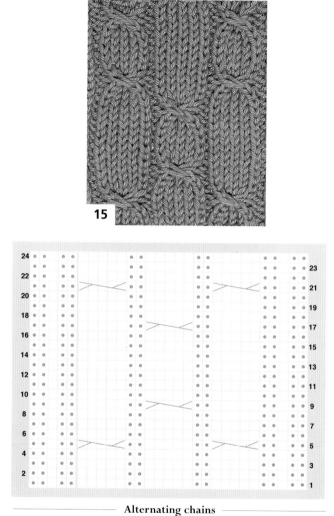

15

Alternating chains

Light-weight cotton, multiple of 24 stitches + 5

The Stitch Collection

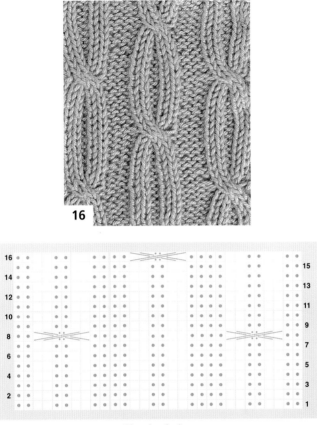

16

Simple chains
4-ply cotton, multiple of 20 stitches + 10

The Stitch Collection

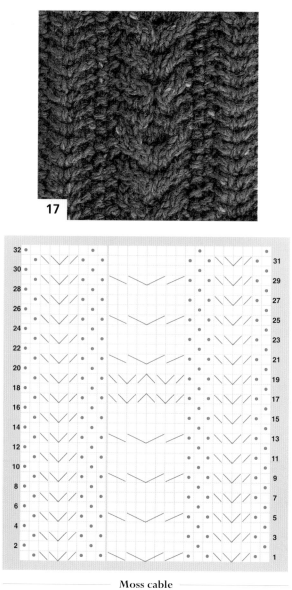

Moss cable

DK tweed, multiple of 17 stitches + 9

The Stitch Collection

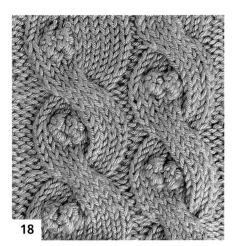

18

Bobble cable

Light-weight cotton, multiple of 26 stitches + 4

The Stitch Collection

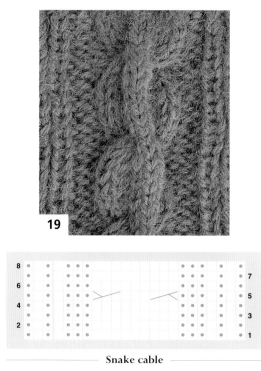

19

Snake cable

Aran-weight mohair, multiple of 20 stitches + 3

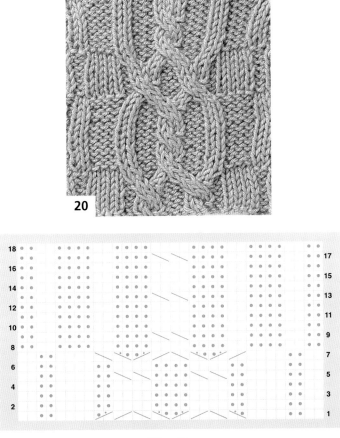

20

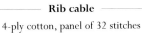

Rib cable

4-ply cotton, panel of 32 stitches

The Stitch Collection

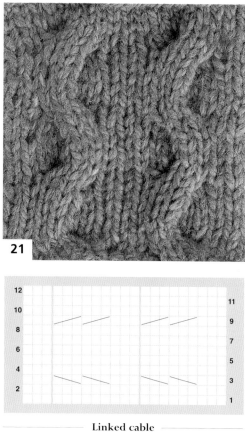

Linked cable

Aran-weight tweed, multiple of 9 stitches + 3

108

22

Double twisted cable
4-ply cotton, multiple of 24 stitches + 8

109

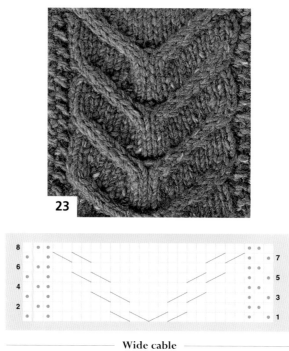

23

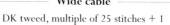

Wide cable

DK tweed, multiple of 25 stitches + 1

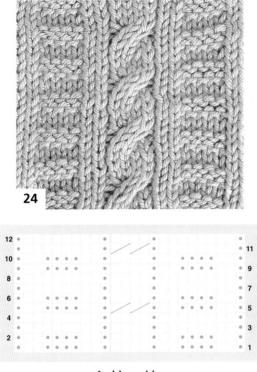

Ladder cable

Medium-weight cotton, multiple of 14 stitches + 10

The Stitch Collection

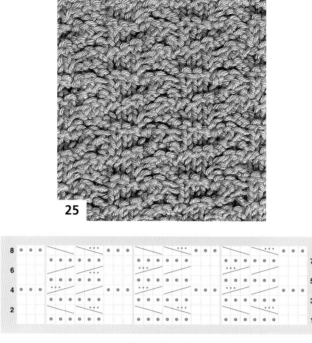

25

Twisted cable

Light-weight cotton, multiple of 9 stitches + 3

The Stitch Collection

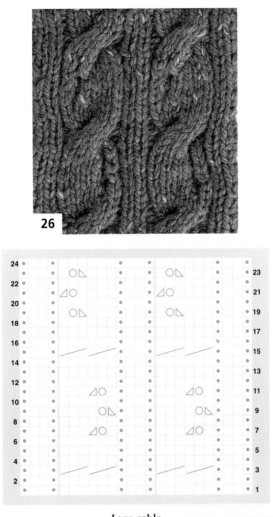

26

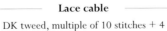

Lace cable

DK tweed, multiple of 10 stitches + 4

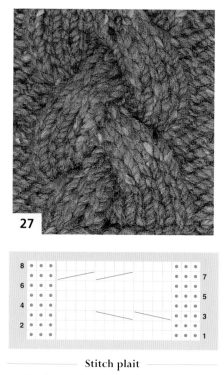

27

Stitch plait

Chunky tweed, multiple of 15 stitches + 3

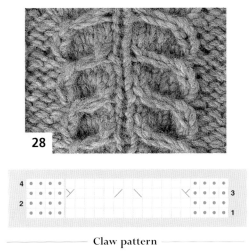

28

Claw pattern

Aran-weight tweed, multiple of 17 stitches + 4

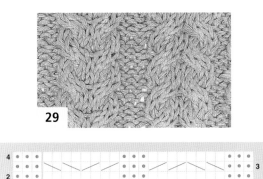

29

Double cable

DK linen, multiple of 22 stitches + 3

The Stitch Collection

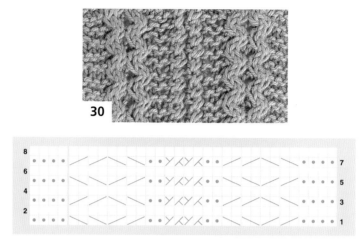

Little pearl cable

4-ply cotton, multiple of 28 stitches + 4

116

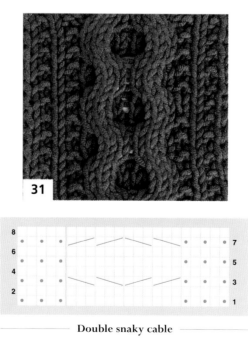

Double snaky cable

Aran-weight cotton, multiple of 17 stitches + 5

The Stitch Collection

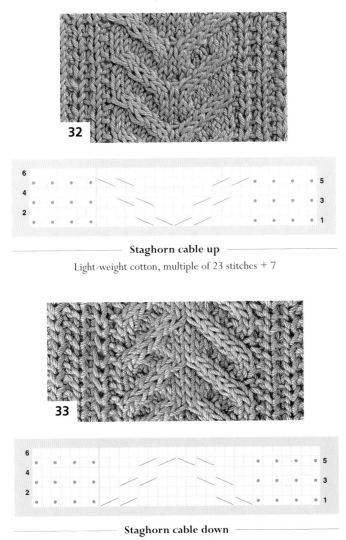

32

Staghorn cable up

Light-weight cotton, multiple of 23 stitches + 7

33

Staghorn cable down

Light-weight cotton, multiple of 23 stitches + 7

The Stitch Collection

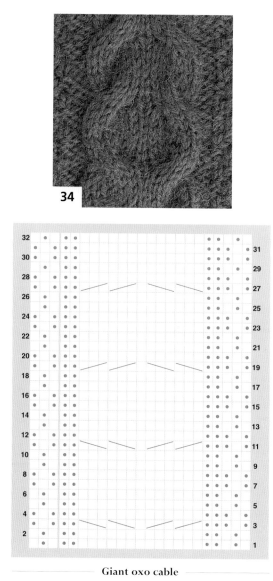

34

Giant oxo cable

Aran-weight mohair, multiple of 20 stitches + 3

The Stitch Collection

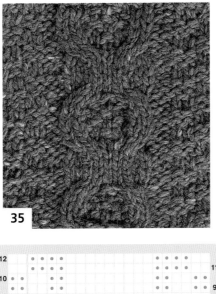

35

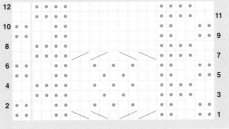

Oxo ripple cable
DK tweed, multiple of 17 stitches + 4

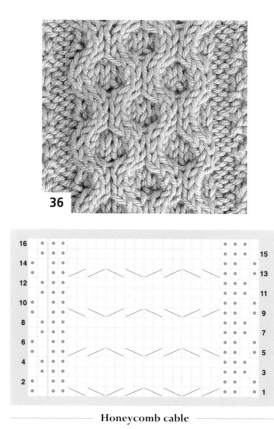

Honeycomb cable

Medium-weight cotton, multiple of 22 stitches + 2

37

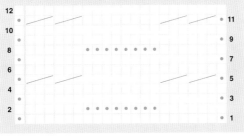

Cable with garter stitch

Aran-weight tweed, multiple of 21 stitches + 1

The Stitch Collection

4

BOBBLE

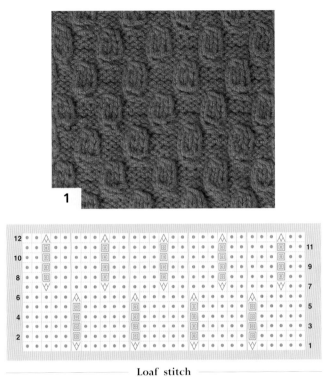

1

Loaf stitch

4-ply cotton, multiple of 6 stitches + 5

The Stitch Collection

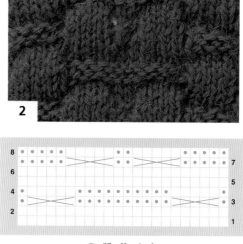

--- **Puffball stitch** ---

Aran-weight mohair, multiple of 22 stitches

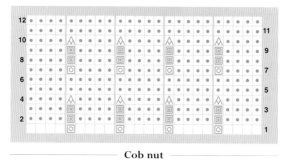

--- **Cob nut** ---

DK linen, multiple of 5 stitches + 4

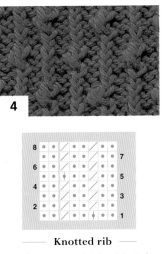

4

————— **Knotted rib** —————

Light-weight cotton, multiple of 6 stitches + 2

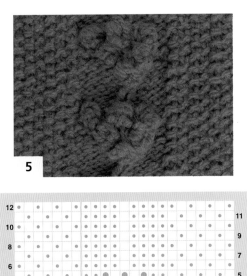

5

————— **Grape design** —————

DK tweed, multiple of 16 stitches + 7

The Stitch Collection

125

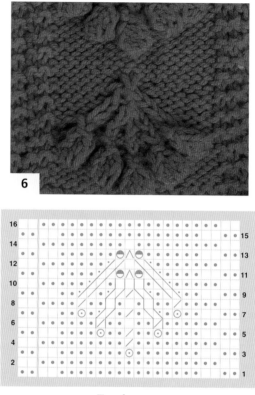

Tassel rowan

Medium-weight cotton, multiple of 21 stitches + 2

126

7

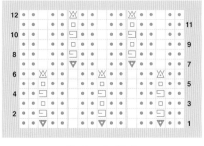

Orchard stitch

Chunky tweed, multiple of 6 stitches + 5

The Stitch Collection

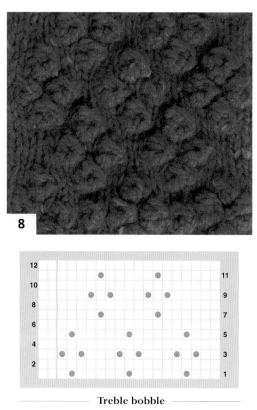

Treble bobble

Chunky tweed, multiple of 17 stitches + 2

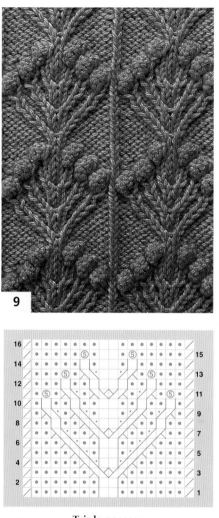

9

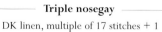

Triple nosegay
DK linen, multiple of 17 stitches + 1

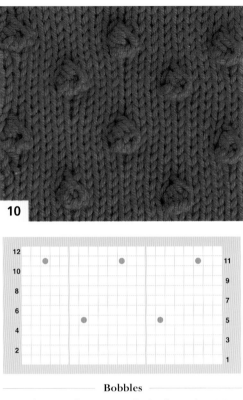

Bobbles

Medium-weight cotton, multiple of 8 stitches + 5

The Stitch Collection

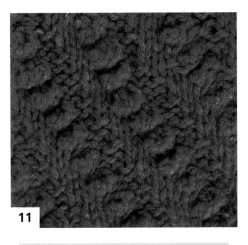

11

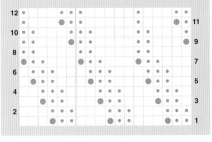

Diagonal bobbles

Aran-weight tweed, multiple of 12 stitches + 6

The Stitch Collection

4

BOBBLE

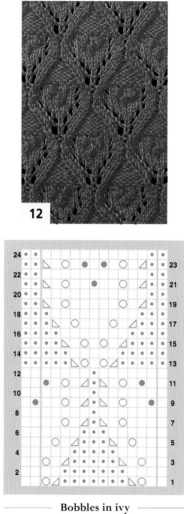

12

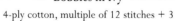

24												
			○		●		●		○		△	|23
22|			○			●			○		△	|21
20|			○						○		△	|19
18|			△	○				○				|17
16|			△	○		○		△				|15
14|					△ ○		○ △					|13
12|						●						
		●	○	△		△	○		●			|11
10|						●						
|●		○	△		△	○			●		|9
8|		○	△		△	○						
						●						|7
6|		○	△		△	○					|5
4|	○	△				△	○				|3
2	○ △						△ ○				1

——— **Bobbles in ivy** ———

4-ply cotton, multiple of 12 stitches + 3

132

The Stitch Collection

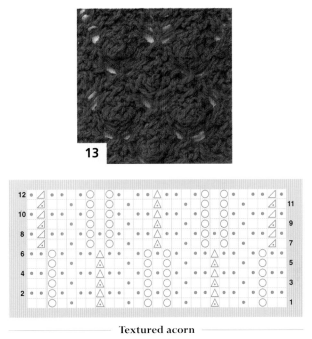

13

Textured acorn

DK tweed, multiple of 25 stitches + 2

The Stitch Collection

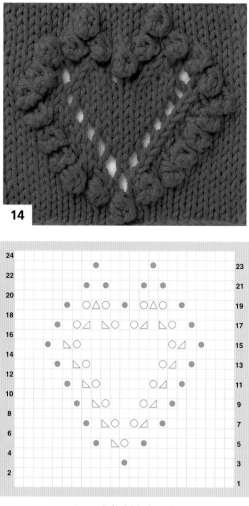

14

Lace & bobble heart
Medium-weight cotton, motif of 23 stitches

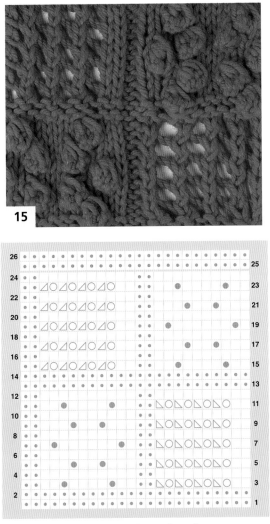

15

Lace & bobble patchwork

Medium-weight cotton, multiple of 24 stitches

The Stitch Collection

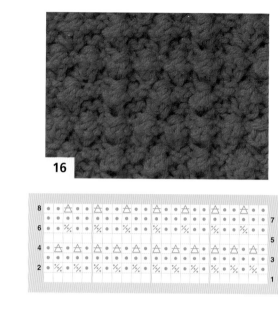

Gooseberry stitch

Medium-weight cotton, multiple of 6 stitches + 5

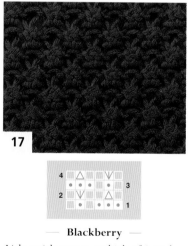

Blackberry

Light-weight cotton, multiple of 4 stitches

The Stitch Collection

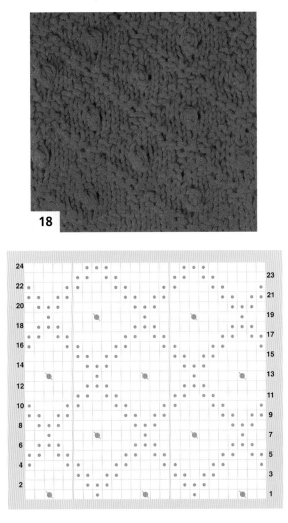

18

Raised diamond

Light-weight cotton, multiple of 10 stitches + 5

The Stitch Collection

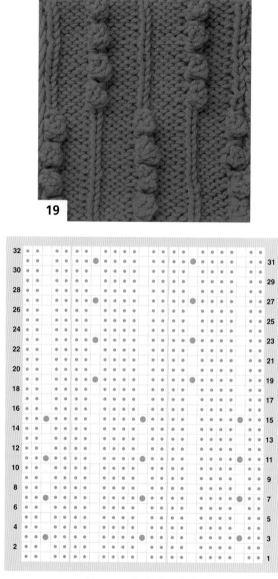

19

Alternate bobble stitch

Light-weight cotton, multiple of 10 stitches + 5

The Stitch Collection

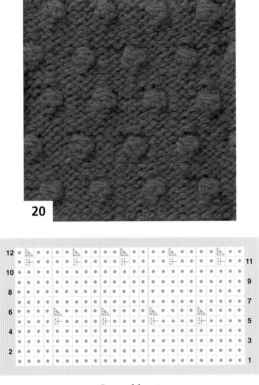

20

Spaced knot

DK tweed, multiple of 5 stitches + 4

The Stitch Collection

4

BOBBLE

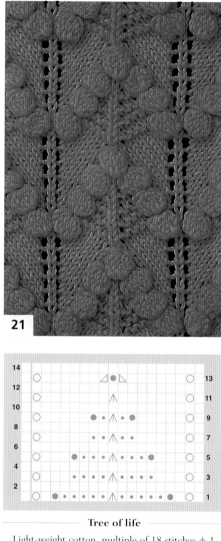

21

Tree of life

Light-weight cotton, multiple of 18 stitches + 1

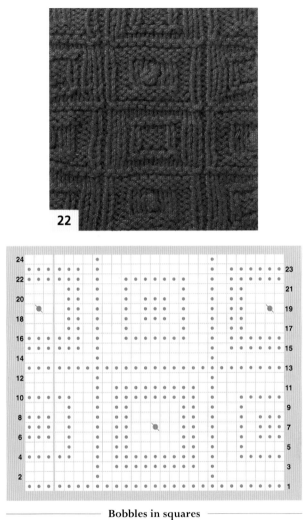

22

Bobbles in squares

4-ply cotton, multiple of 24 stitches + 3

The Stitch Collection

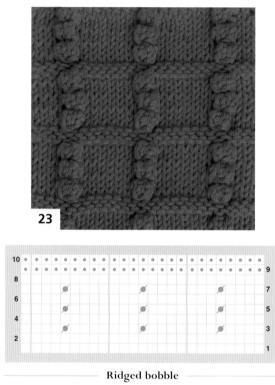

23

Ridged bobble

Light-weight cotton, multiple of 8 stitches + 1

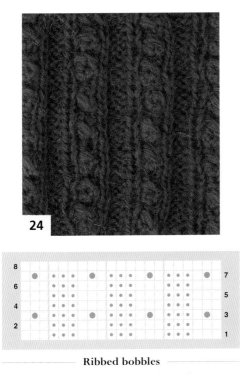

24

| | | | | | | | | | | | | | | | | | | | |
|8| |●| |●|●|●| |●| |●|●|●| |●| |●|●|●| |●|7|

Ribbed bobbles

Aran-weight mohair, multiple of 6 stitches + 3

BOBBLE

4

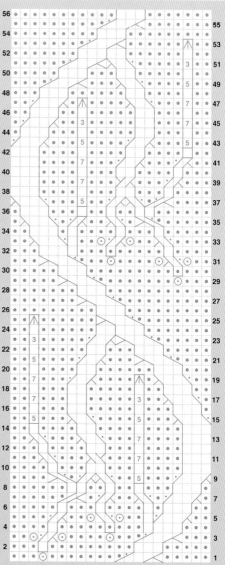

25

Working a leaf

Row 9: $\boxed{5}$ = k1, yo, k1, yo, k1 into stitch; in next row p5

Row 11: $\boxed{7}$ = k2, yo, k1, yo, k2; in next row p7

Row 13: = k7; in next row p7

Row 15: = skpo, k3, k2tog; in next row p5

Row 17: = skpo, k1, k2tog; in next row p3

Repeat this series of instructions in all other areas.

144

—— **Celtic vine** ——

Medium-weight cotton, panel of 21 stitches

T h e   S t i t c h   C o l l e c t i o n

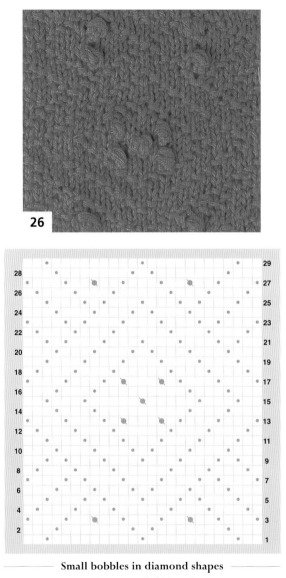

26

Small bobbles in diamond shapes

DK linen, motif of 25 stitches

4

BOBBLE

145

The Stitch Collection

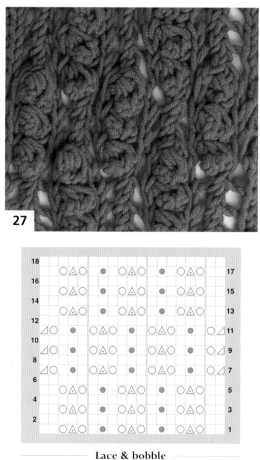

27

Lace & bobble

Aran-weight cotton, multiple of 6 stitches + 7

5

LACE

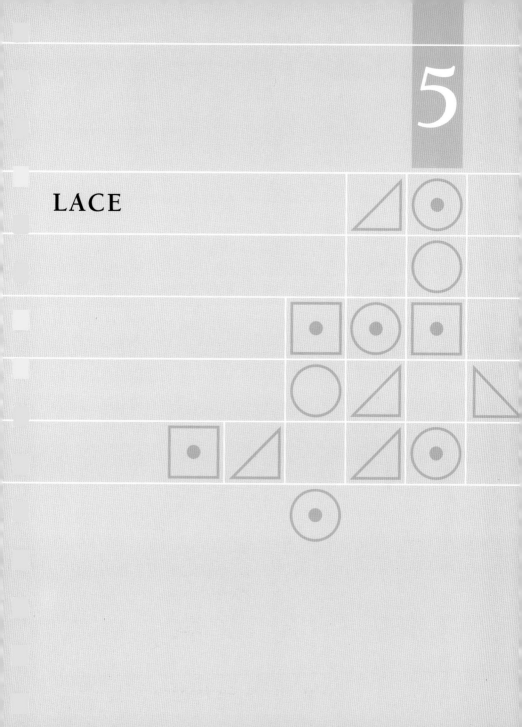

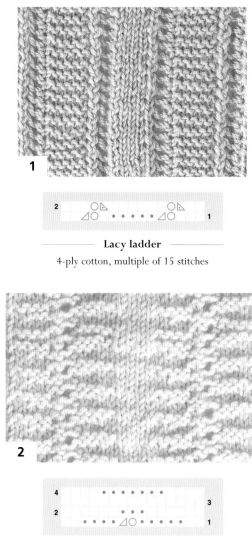

1

Lacy ladder

4-ply cotton, multiple of 15 stitches

2

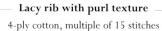

Lacy rib with purl texture

4-ply cotton, multiple of 15 stitches

The Stitch Collection

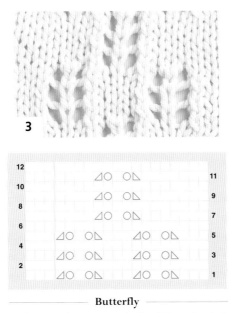

3

12									
				⊿O OⱯ					11
10									
				⊿O OⱯ					9
8									
				⊿O OⱯ					7
6									
	⊿O OⱯ		⊿O OⱯ					5
4									
	⊿O OⱯ		⊿O OⱯ					3
2									
	⊿O OⱯ		⊿O OⱯ					1

Butterfly

Medium-weight cotton, multiple of 16 stitches + 3

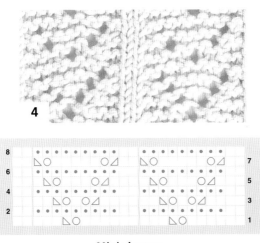

4

149

8	• • • • • •			• • • • • •		
	Ɐ O O ⊿			Ɐ O O ⊿		7
6	• • • • • • • •			• • • • • • • •		
	Ɐ O O ⊿			Ɐ O O ⊿		5
4	• • • • • • • • • •			• • • • • • • • • •		
	Ɐ O O ⊿			Ɐ O O ⊿		3
2	• • • • • • • • • • • •			• • • • • • • • • • • •		
	Ɐ O			Ɐ O		1

Mini chevron

DK wool cotton, multiple of 11 stitches + 2

The Stitch Collection

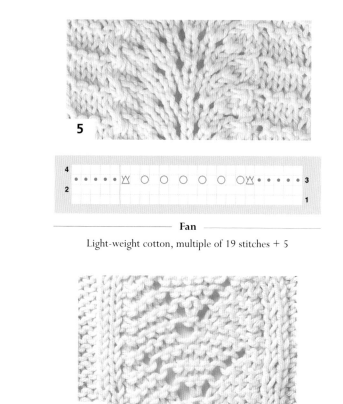

Fan

Light-weight cotton, multiple of 19 stitches + 5

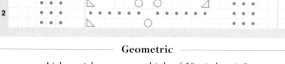

Geometric

Light-weight cotton, multiple of 20 stitches + 9

The Stitch Collection

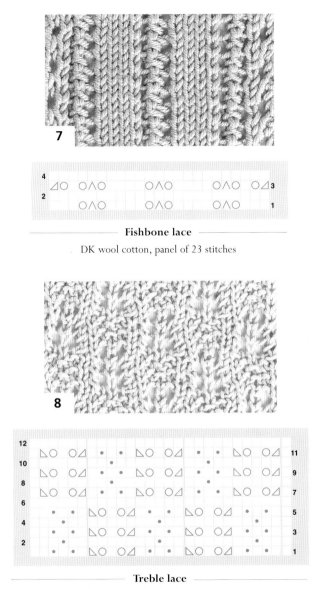

7

4							
2	⊿O	O∧O		O∧O		O∧O O⊿	3
		O∧O		O∧O		O∧O	1

Fishbone lace

DK wool cotton, panel of 23 stitches

8

12												
	◣O O⊿	• •	◣O O⊿	• •	◣O O⊿	11
10						
	◣O O⊿	• •	◣O O⊿	• •	◣O O⊿	9
8		•		•		
	◣O O⊿	• •	◣O O⊿	• •	◣O O⊿	7
6						
	• •	◣O O⊿	• •	◣O O⊿	• •	5
4	•				•	
	• •	◣O O⊿	• •	◣O O⊿	• •	3
2		•		•		
	• •	◣O O⊿	• •	◣O O⊿	• •	1

Treble lace

4-ply cotton, multiple of 10 stitches + 7

The Stitch Collection

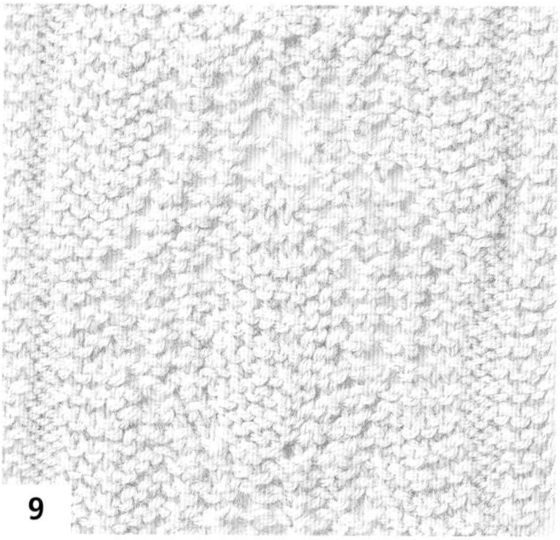

9

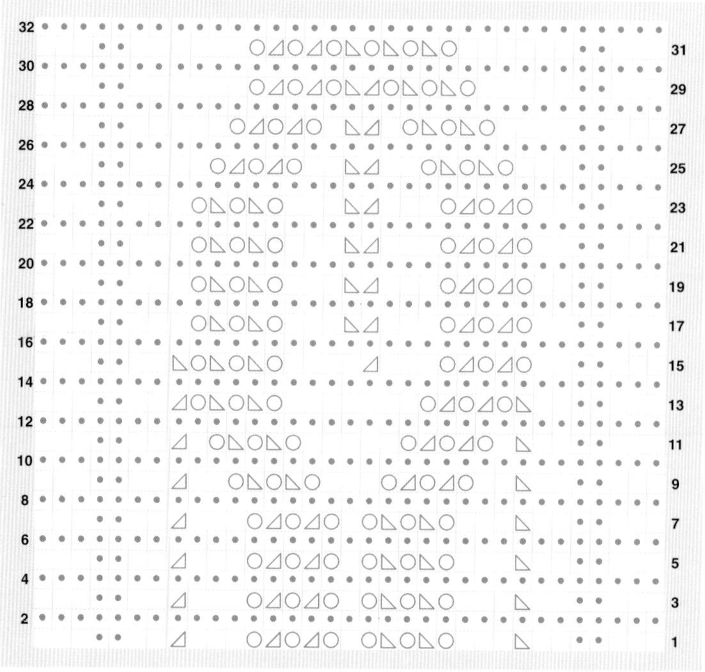

32																								

Leaf

4-ply cotton, multiple of 26 stitches + 7

The Stitch Collection

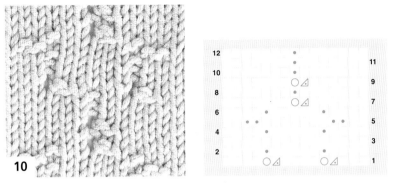

10

Eyelet moving lace

Aran-weight cotton, multiple of 11 stitches + 4

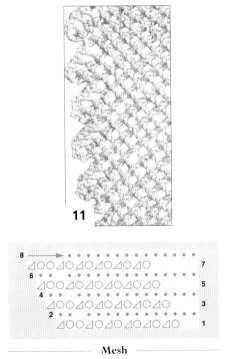

11

Mesh

Light-weight cotton, edging of 14 stitches increasing to 18,
multiple of 8 rows

The Stitch Collection

12

Knitting chart (rows 1–48):

Left	Right
48	47
46	45
44	43
42	41
40	39
38	37
36	35
34	33
32	31
30	29
28	27
26	25
24	23
22	21
20	19
18	17
16	15
14	13
12	11
10	9
8	7
6	5
4	3
2	1

Falling leaves

Light-weight cotton, multiple of 16 stitches + 1,
at the end of the last pattern repeat knit 2 together instead of 3

The Stitch Collection

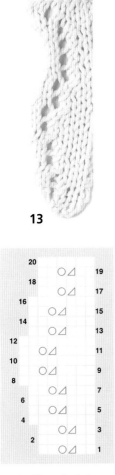

13

20					19
18			O△		17
16			O△		15
14			O△		13
12		O△			11
10		O△			9
8		O△			7
6		O△			5
4			O△		3
2			O△		1

— **Scalloped edging** —

Light-weight cotton,
edging of 6 stitches increasing to 8,
multiple of 20 rows

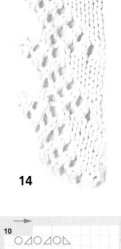

14

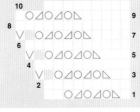

10	O△O△O△		9
8	V O△O△O△		7
6	V O△O△O△		5
4	V O△O△O△		3
2	O△O△O△		1

— **Zigzag edging** —

Light-weight cotton,
edging of 9 stitches increasing to 12,
multiple of 10 rows

5

LACE

155

The Stitch Collection

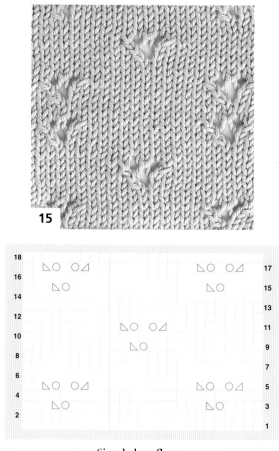

15

Simple lace flower

Light-weight cotton, multiple of 16 stitches + 9

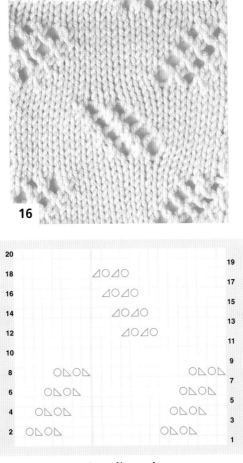

16

20															
18				◿O◿O											19
16				◿O◿O											17
14				◿O◿O											15
12				◿O◿O											13
10															11
8		O◺O◺					O◺O◺							9
6		O◺O◺					O◺O◺							7
4	O◺O◺						O◺O◺							5
2	O◺O◺						O◺O◺							3
															1

Lace diagonal

DK wool cotton, multiple of 14 stitches + 8

The Stitch Collection

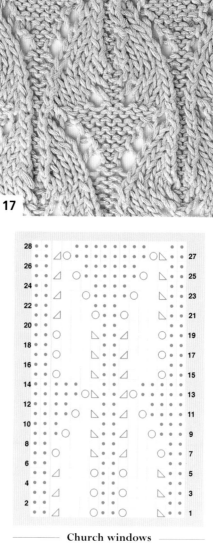

17

Church windows

DK linen, multiple of 14 stitches + 2

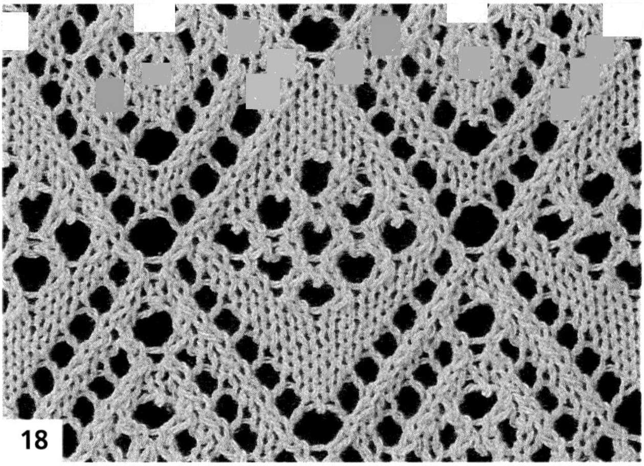

18

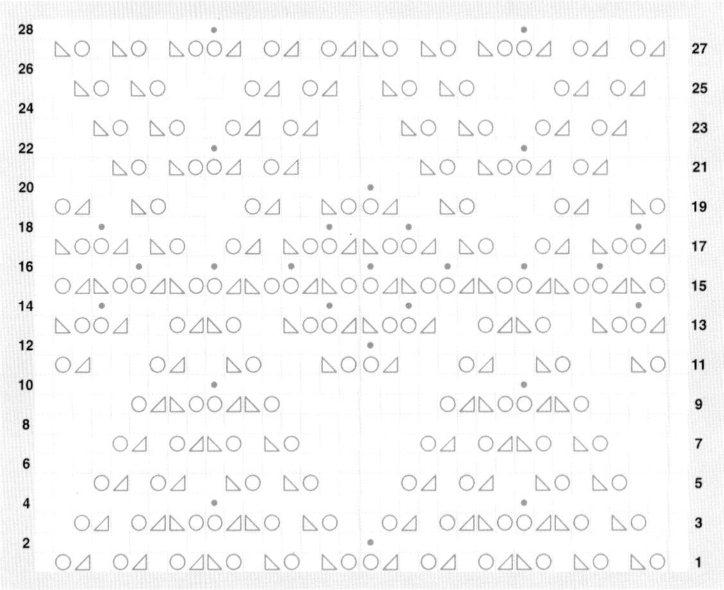

Feminine diamonds

Light-weight cotton, multiple of 16 stitches + 18

The Stitch Collection

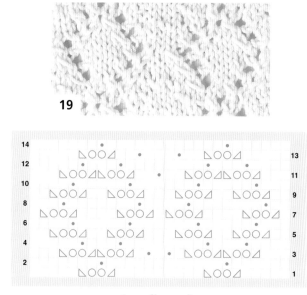

19

─── **Lace diamonds** ───

Light-weight cotton, multiple of 13 stitches + 14

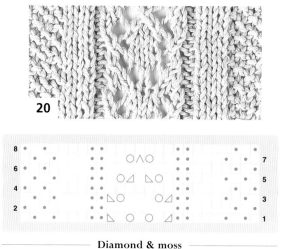

20

─── **Diamond & moss** ───

DK linen, multiple of 25 stitches

The Stitch Collection

21

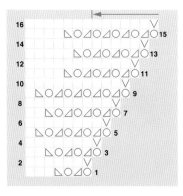

─────── **Treble lace edging** ───────

Light-weight cotton, edging of 7 stitches increasing to 14,
multiple of 16 rows

The Stitch Collection

5

L A C E

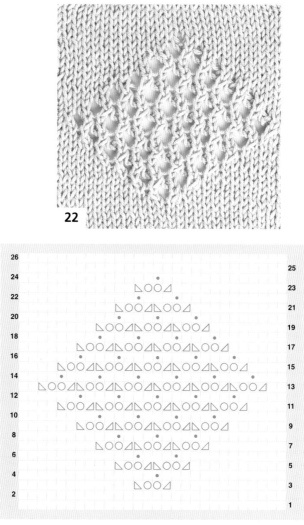

22

162

Eyelet diamonds

4-ply cotton, motif of 28 stitches

23

28	⋅ ⋅	
	∆OO∧OO⊿	27
26	⋅ ⋅	
	∆OO⊿ ∆OO⊿	25
24 ⋅ ⋅ ⋅ ⋅		
⋅ ⋅ ⋅	∆OO⊿ ∆OO⊿	23
22 ⋅ ⋅ ⋅ ⋅		
⋅ ⋅ ⋅	∆OO⊿ ∆OO⊿	21
20 ⋅ ⋅ ⋅ ⋅		
⋅ ⋅ ⋅	∆OO⊿ ∆OO⊿	19
18		
	∆OO⊿ ∆OO⊿	17
16	⋅ ⋅	
	∆OO∧OO⊿	15
14 ⋅ ⋅		
∆OO∧OO⊿		13
12 ⋅ ⋅		
∆OO⊿ ∆OO⊿		11
10 ⋅ ⋅	⋅ ⋅ ⋅ ⋅	
∆OO⊿ ∆OO⊿	⋅ ⋅ ⋅	9
8 ⋅ ⋅	⋅ ⋅ ⋅ ⋅	
∆OO⊿ ∆OO⊿	⋅ ⋅ ⋅	7
6 ⋅ ⋅	⋅ ⋅ ⋅ ⋅	
∆OO⊿ ∆OO⊿		5
4 ⋅ ⋅		
∆OO⊿ ∆OO⊿		3
2 ⋅ ⋅		
∆OO∧OO⊿		1

Alternating diamonds

DK wool cotton, multiple of 26 stitches

163

The Stitch Collection

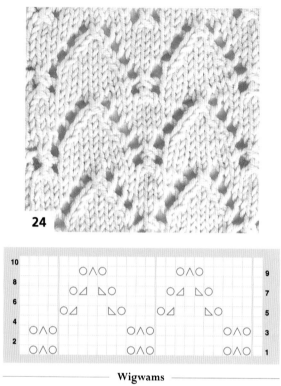

24

10										
			O∧O			O∧O			9
8		O⊿	⊾O		O⊿	⊾O			7
6										
	O⊿		⊾O		O⊿		⊾O		5
4										
O∧O			O∧O			O∧O		3	
2										
O∧O			O∧O			O∧O		1	

Wigwams

DK wool cotton, multiple of 10 stitches + 5

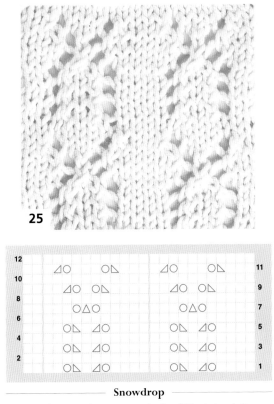

25

12										
10		⊿O	O◣		⊿O	O◣				11
8		⊿O O◣			⊿O O◣					9
6		O△O			O△O					7
4		O◣ ⊿O			O◣ ⊿O					5
2		O◣ ⊿O			O◣ ⊿O					3
		O◣ ⊿O			O◣ ⊿O					1

Snowdrop

Medium-weight cotton, multiple of 11 stitches + 2

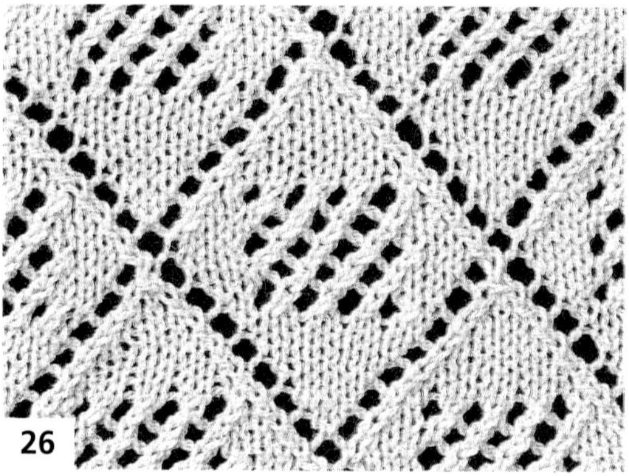

26

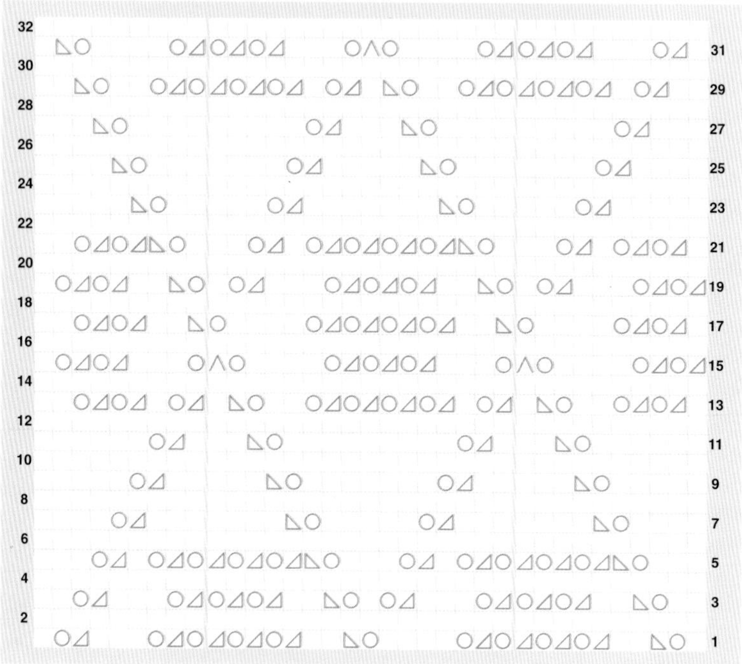

Lace squares in diamonds

Light-weight cotton, multiple of 16 stitches + 19

The Stitch Collection

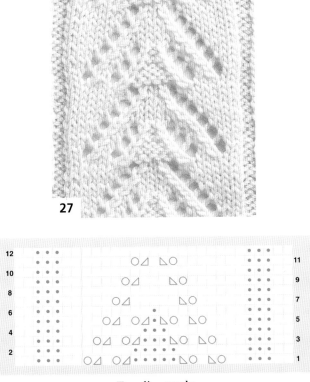

27

12			11
10			9
8			7
6			5
4			3
2			1

Traveling tracks

4-ply cotton, multiple of 22 stitches + 7

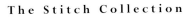

The Stitch Collection

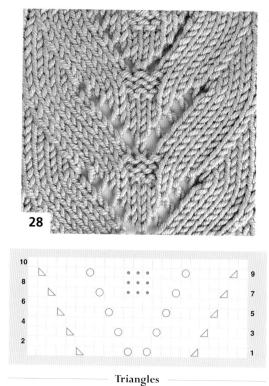

28

Triangles

DK wool cotton, multiple of 23 stitches

168

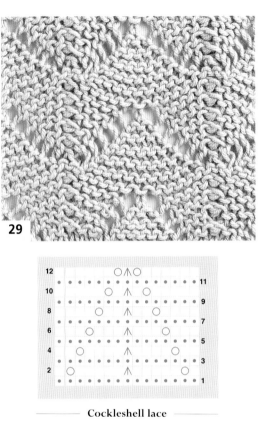

29

Cockleshell lace

4-ply cotton, multiple of 14 stitches + 1

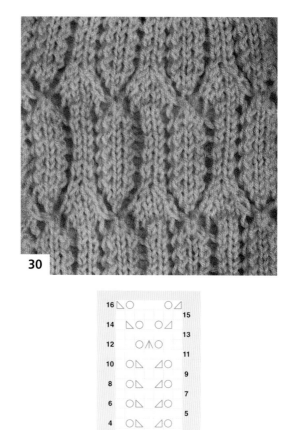

Delicate lace

4-ply cotton, multiple of 7 stitches

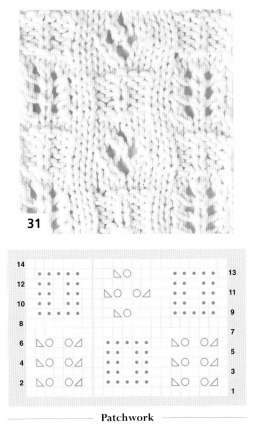

31

Patchwork

Medium-weight cotton, multiple of 14 stitches + 7

The Stitch Collection

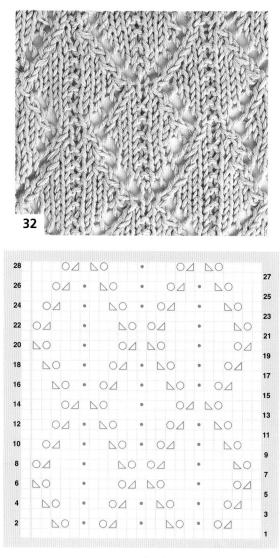

Lace wheels

DK linen, multiple of 24 stitches + 1

172

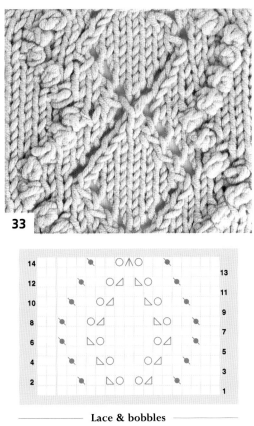

33

14 · ○∧○ · 13
12 · ○⊿ ⊿○ · 11
10 · ○⊿ ⊿○ · 9
8 · ○⊿ ⊿○ · 7
6 · ⊿○ ○⊿ · 5
4 · ⊿○ ○⊿ · 3
2 · ⊿○ ○⊿ · 1

Lace & bobbles

Aran-weight cotton, multiple of 17 stitches + 2

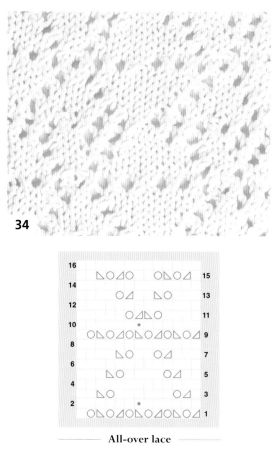

34

All-over lace

Light-weight cotton, multiple of 13 stitches

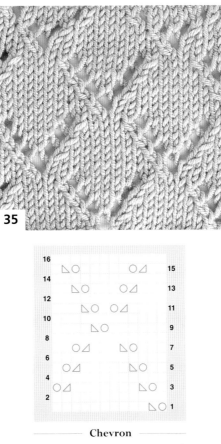

35

16							
	◺O			O◿		15
14							
		◺O			O◿	13
12							
			◺O	O◿		11
10							
			◺O			9
8							
		O◿		◺O		7
6							
	O◿			◺O		5
4							
	O◿				◺O	3
2							
					◺O	1

——— **Chevron** ———

DK wool cotton, multiple of 12 stitches

175

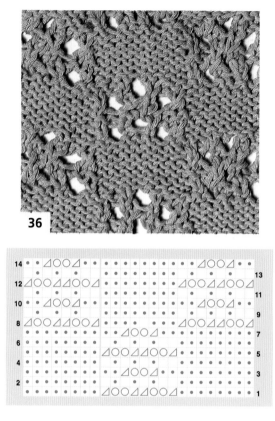

36

Lacy tiles

DK linen, multiple of 16 stitches + 8

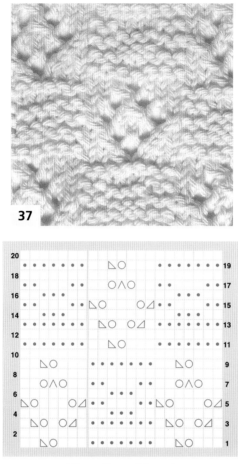

37

Alternating patchwork

DK wool cotton, multiple of 14 stitches + 7

The Stitch Collection

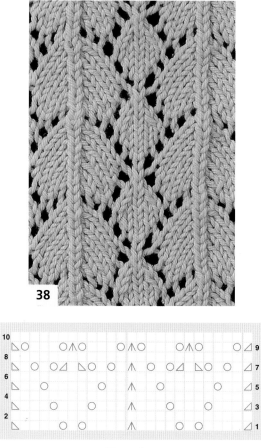

Horseshoe

Light-weight cotton, multiple of 12 stitches + 13

178

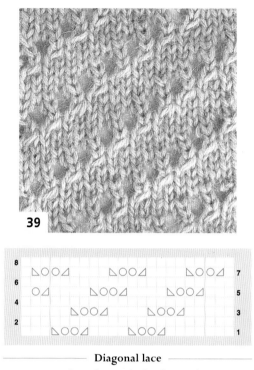

39

8		Λ	O	O	⊿				Λ	O	O	⊿				Λ	O	O	⊿		7
6			O	⊿				Λ	O	O	⊿				Λ	O	O	⊿			5
4				Λ	O	O	⊿				Λ	O	O	⊿							3
2					Λ	O	O	⊿					Λ	O	O	⊿					1

Diagonal lace

Aran-weight mohair, multiple of 16 stitches + 6

The Stitch Collection

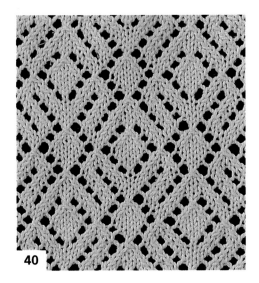

40

28																													27
26		O⊿	⊾O		O⊿	⊾O		O⊿	⊾O		O⊿	⊾O																	27
24	⊾O	⊾O	⊾O		O⊿	O⊿	O∧O	⊾O	⊾O		O⊿	O⊿	O⊿																25
22	⊾O	⊾O			O⊿	O⊿	⊾O	⊾O			O⊿	O⊿																	23
20		⊾O	⊾O		O⊿	O⊿		⊾O	⊾O		O⊿	O⊿																	21
18		O⊿	O∧O		O⊿	O∧O	⊾O		O∧O	⊾O																			19
16		O⊿	O⊿	⊾O		O⊿	⊾O		O⊿	⊾O	⊾O																		17
14	⊾O	⊾O			O∧O			O∧O			O⊿	O⊿																	15
12	⊾O	⊾O			O⊿	⊾O		O⊿	⊾O		O⊿	O⊿																	13
10		O⊿	O∧O	⊾O	⊾O	O⊿	O⊿	O∧O	⊾O																				11
8		O⊿	O⊿	⊾O	⊾O			O⊿	O⊿	⊾O	⊾O																		9
6		O⊿	O⊿		⊾O	⊾O		O⊿	O⊿		⊾O	⊾O																	7
4	⊾O		O⊿	O∧O	⊾O		O∧O		O⊿	O∧O	⊾O		O⊿																5
2	⊾O		O⊿		⊾O			O⊿	⊾O		O⊿	⊾O		O⊿															3
	O∧O			O∧O			O∧O			O∧O																			1

Interlocking diamonds

4-ply cotton, multiple of 16 stitches + 19

FAIR ISLE

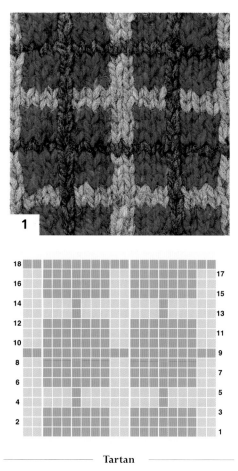

Tartan

Aran-weight wool, multiple of 9 stitches + 2

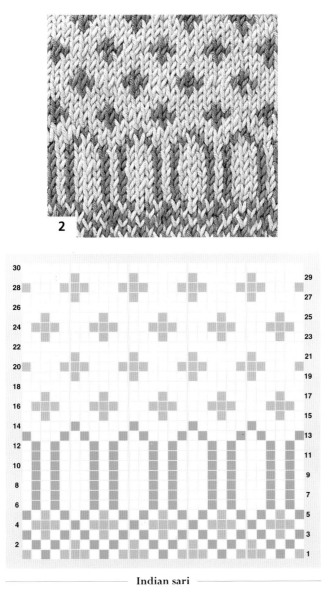

Indian sari

Light-weight cotton, multiple of 6 stitches + 5

The Stitch Collection

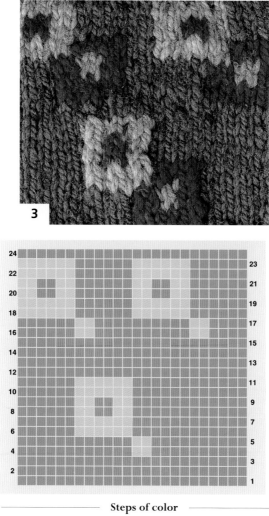

3

—————— **Steps of color** ——————

Aran-weight wool, multiple of 24 stitches

The Stitch Collection

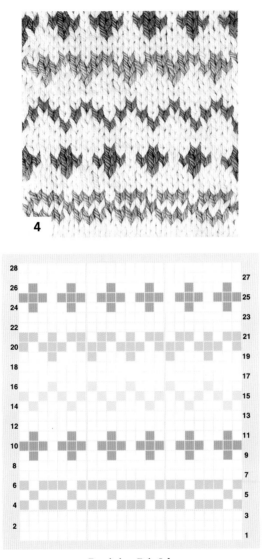

4

Feminine Fair Isle

Medium-weight cotton, multiple of 8 stitches + 7,
multiple of 25 rows + 3

The Stitch Collection

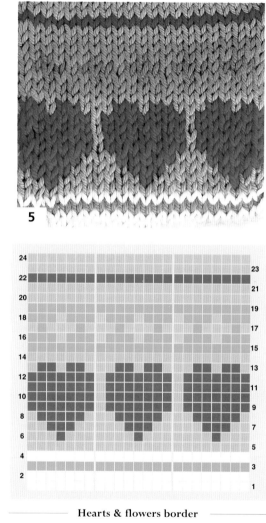

Hearts & flowers border

Medium-weight cotton, multiple of 8 stitches + 7

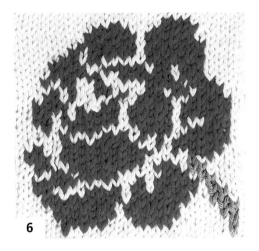

6

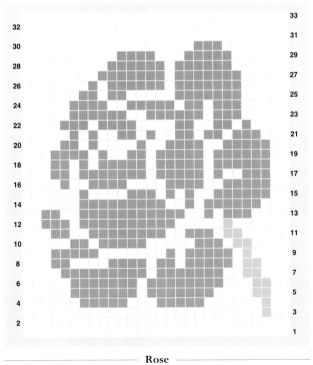

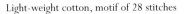

Rose

Light-weight cotton, motif of 28 stitches

The Stitch Collection

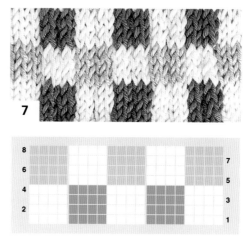

Gingham

Light-weight cotton, multiple of 8 stitches + 4

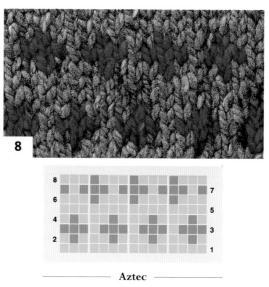

Aztec

Chunky tweed, multiple of 4 stitches + 3

The Stitch Collection

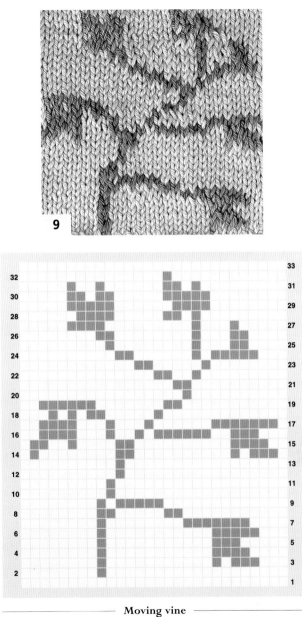

9

Moving vine

Light-weight cotton, motif of 28 stitches

The Stitch Collection

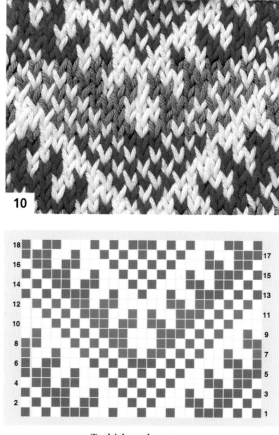

Turkish sock pattern

Light-weight cotton, multiple of 24 stitches + 1

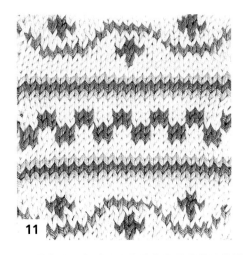

11

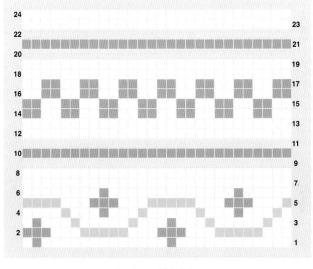

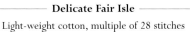

— **Delicate Fair Isle** —
Light-weight cotton, multiple of 28 stitches

The Stitch Collection

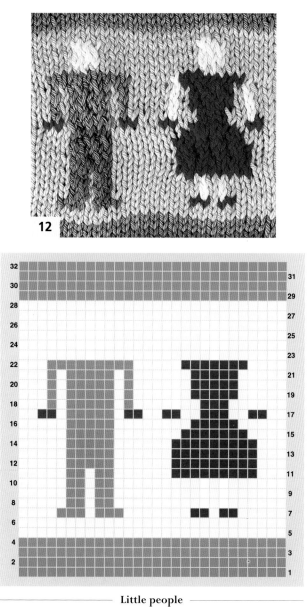

Little people

Light-weight cotton, motif of 28 stitches

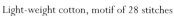

The Stitch Collection

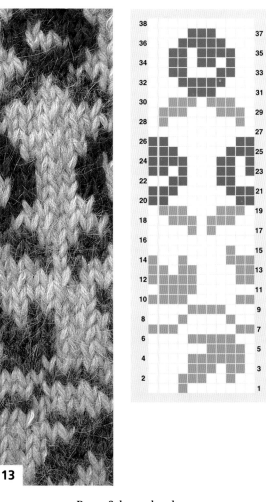

Roses & leaves border

Aran-weight mohair, multiple of 10 stitches + 1

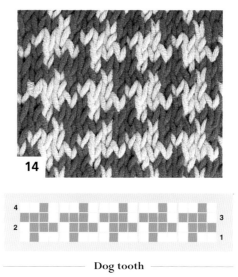

14

--------- **Dog tooth** ---------

Aran-weight cotton, multiple of 4 stitches

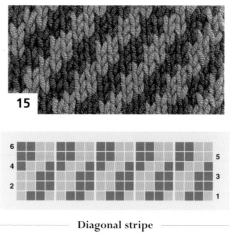

15

--------- **Diagonal stripe** ---------

Aran-weight cotton, multiple of 4 stitches

The Stitch Collection

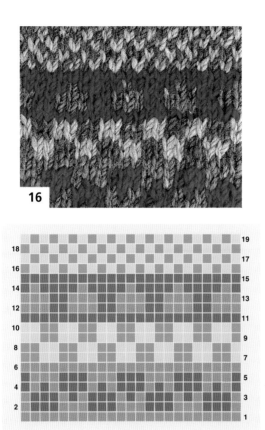

Traditional

DK tweed, rows 1–6 multiple of 6 stitches,
rows 7–10 multiple of 4 stitches,

rows 11–15 multiple of 5 stitches,

rows 16–19 multiple of 2 stitches

195

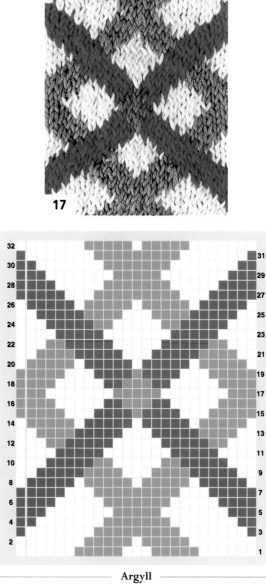

17

Argyll

Light-weight cotton, multiple of 24 stitches + 1

The Stitch Collection

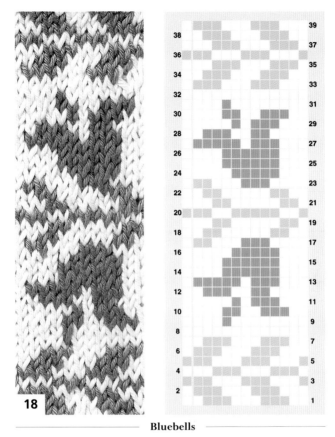

Bluebells

Light-weight cotton, multiple of 12 stitches + 1

The Stitch Collection

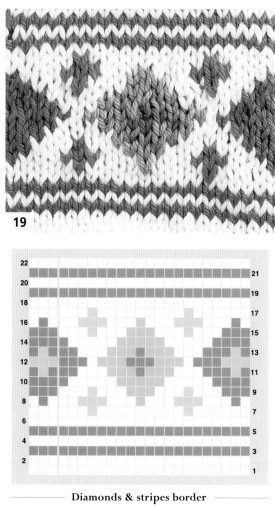

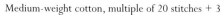

Diamonds & stripes border

Medium-weight cotton, multiple of 20 stitches + 3

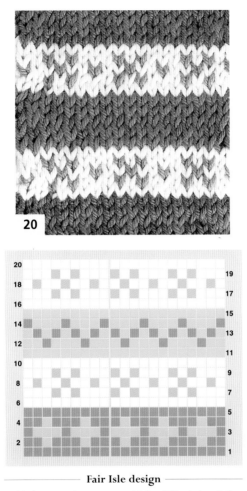

Fair Isle design

Medium-weight cotton, multiple of 12 stitches + 9

The Stitch Collection

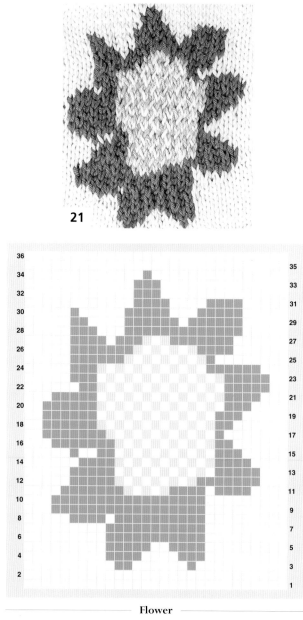

21

Flower

Light-weight cotton, motif of 29 stitches

The Stitch Collection

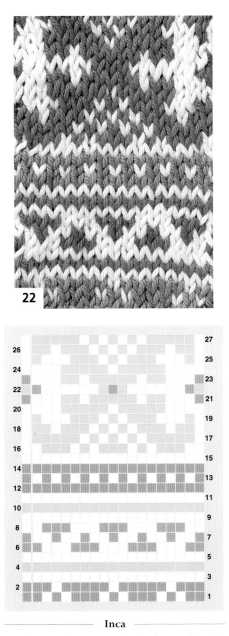

Inca

Medium-weight cotton, multiple of 18 stitches + 1

The Stitch Collection

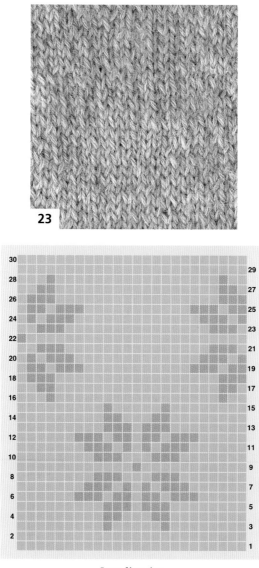

23

Scandinavian

Aran-weight mohair, multiple of 23 stitches – 1

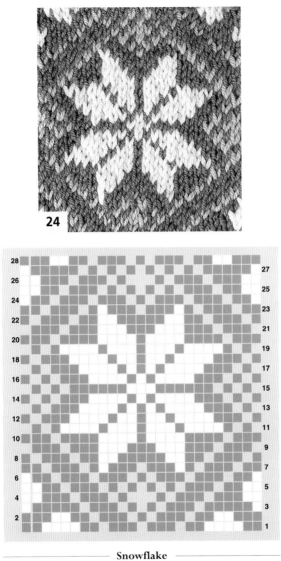

24

Snowflake

DK wool cotton, multiple of 24 stitches + 1

The Stitch Collection

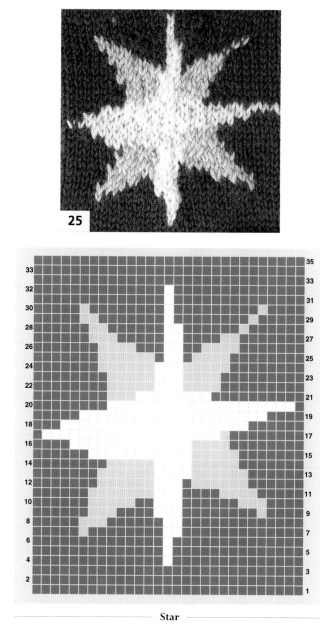

25

Star
4-ply wool, motif of 29 stitches

The Stitch Collection

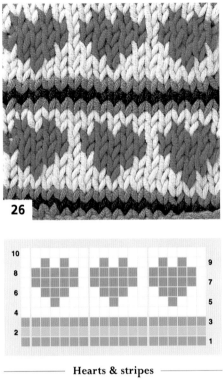

26

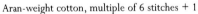

Hearts & stripes

Aran-weight cotton, multiple of 6 stitches + 1

The Stitch Collection

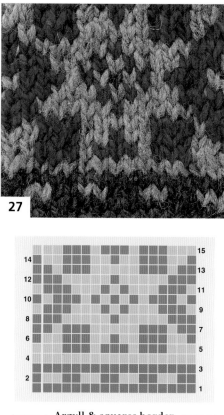

27

Argyll & squares border

DK tweed, multiple of 16 stitches + 1

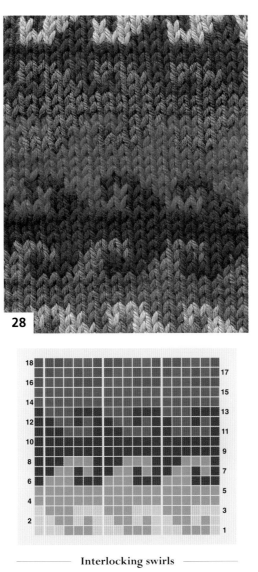

Interlocking swirls

Light-weight cotton, multiple of 6 stitches + 1

The Stitch Collection

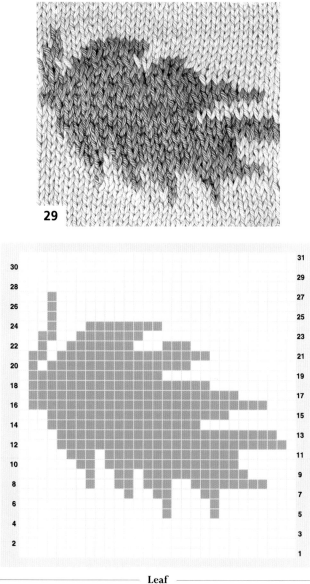

Leaf

Light-weight cotton, motif of 29 stitches

The Stitch Collection

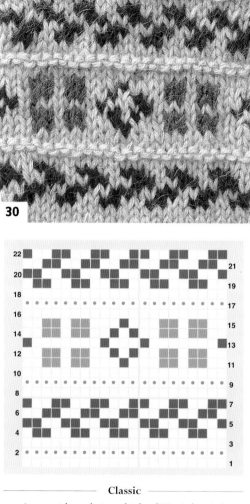

Classic

Aran-weight mohair, multiple of 12 stitches + 9,
multiple of 15 rows + 7

The Stitch Collection

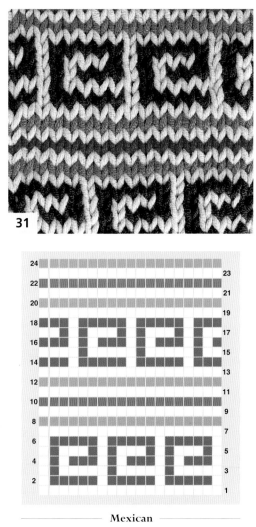

Mexican

Aran-weight cotton, multiple of 18 stitches + 1

The Stitch Collection

32

Norwegian

DK wool cotton, multiple of 24 stitches + 1

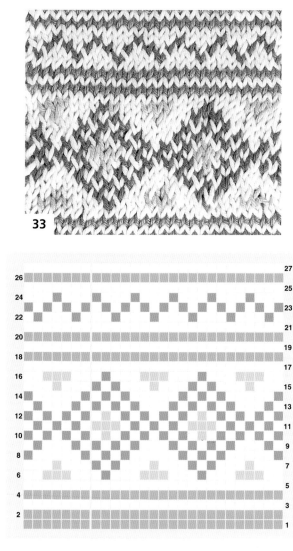

33

Checkered diamond border

Light-weight cotton, multiple of 20 stitches + 7

The Stitch Collection

7

INTARSIA

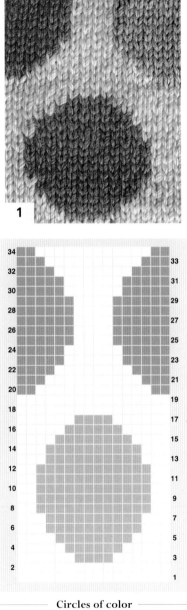

1

Circles of color

4-ply cotton, multiple of 16 stitches

The Stitch Collection

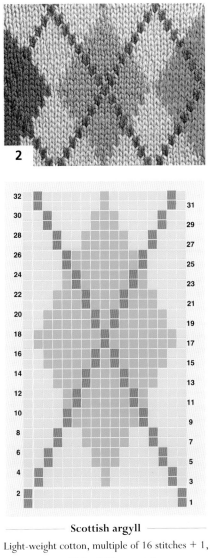

2

Scottish argyll

Light-weight cotton, multiple of 16 stitches + 1,
multiple of 30 rows + 2

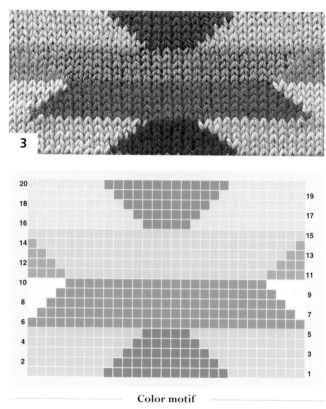

Color motif

Light-weight cotton, motif of 29 stitches

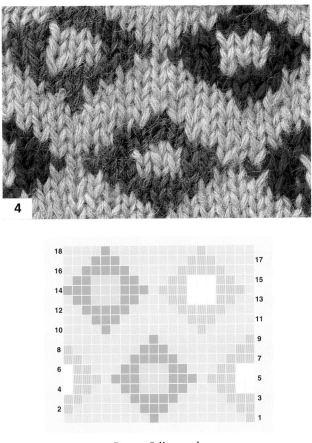

Rows of diamonds

Aran-weight mohair, multiple of 20 stitches

The Stitch Collection

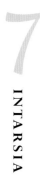

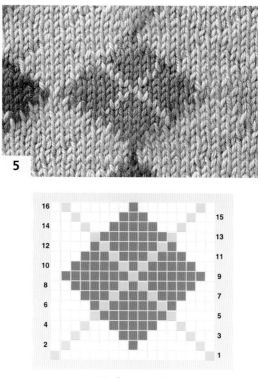

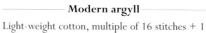

Modern argyll

Light-weight cotton, multiple of 16 stitches + 1

The Stitch Collection

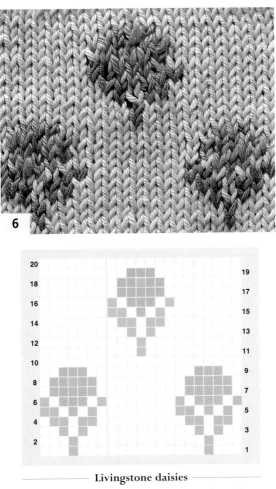

Livingstone daisies

Light-weight cotton, multiple of 14 stitches + 7

The Stitch Collection

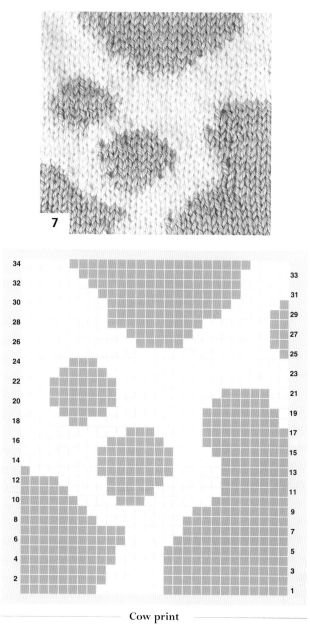

Cow print

4-ply wool, motif of 28 stitches

The Stitch Collection

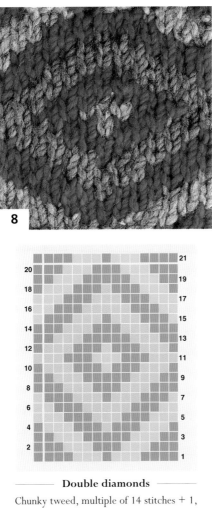

Double diamonds

Chunky tweed, multiple of 14 stitches + 1,
multiple of 20 rows + 1

The Stitch Collection

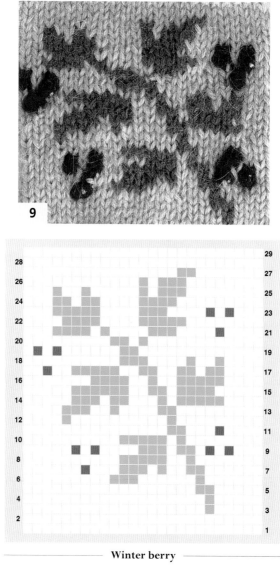

9

— Winter berry —

Aran-weight mohair, motif of 25 stitches

The Stitch Collection

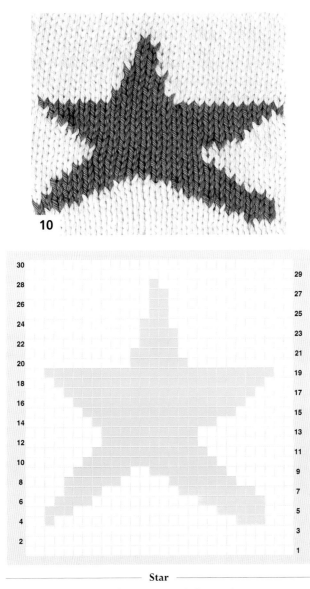

10

— **Star** —

Light-weight cotton, motif of 28 stitches

The Stitch Collection

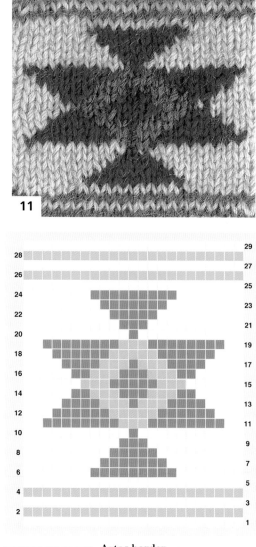

11

— **Aztec border** —
Aran-weight mohair, multiple of 23 stitches

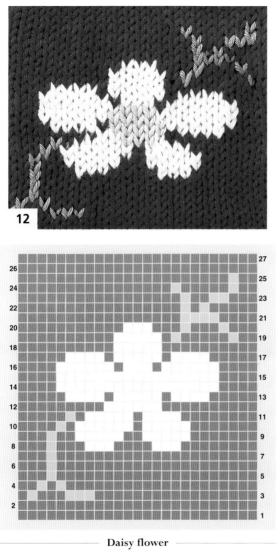

Daisy flower

Light-weight cotton, multiple of 25 stitches

The Stitch Collection

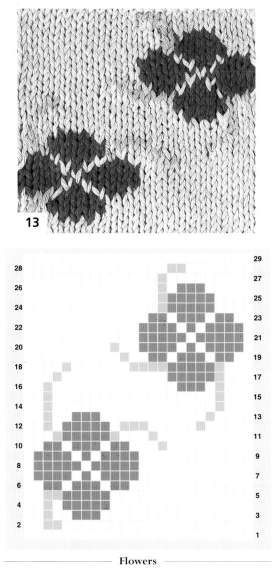

Flowers

DK linen, multiple of 24 stitches

The Stitch Collection

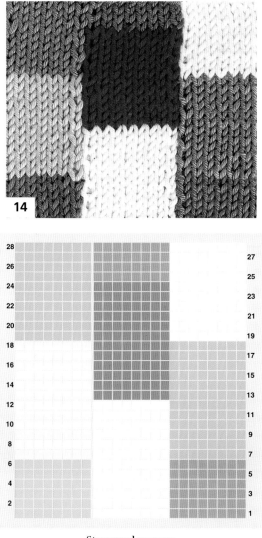

Staggered squares

Light-weight cotton, multiple of 16 stitches + 8

The Stitch Collection

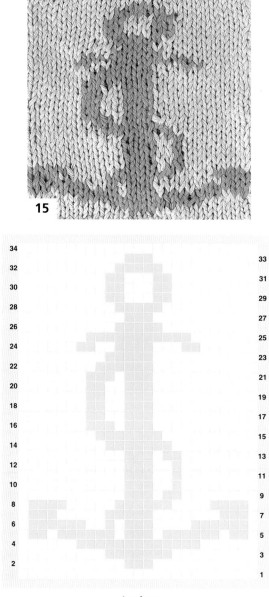

15

Anchor

DK linen, motif of 25 stitches

The Stitch Collection

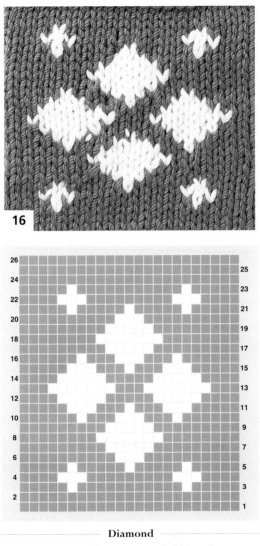

16

Diamond

Medium-weight cotton, motif of 23 stitches

The Stitch Collection

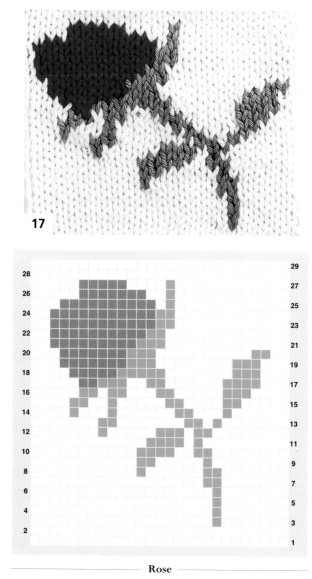

17

Rose

Light-weight cotton, motif of 27 stitches

The Stitch Collection

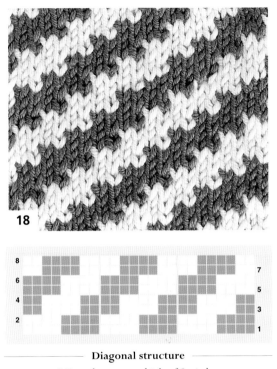

18

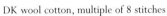

Diagonal structure

DK wool cotton, multiple of 8 stitches

The Stitch Collection

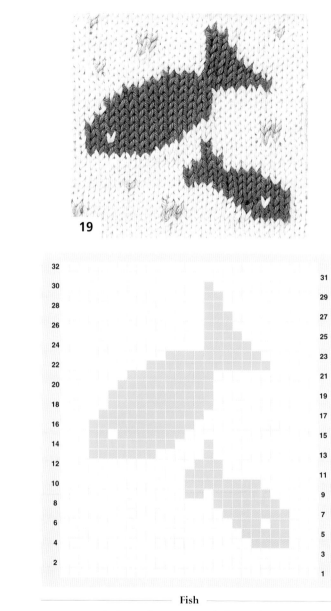

19

Fish

Light-weight cotton, motif of 27 stitches

The Stitch Collection

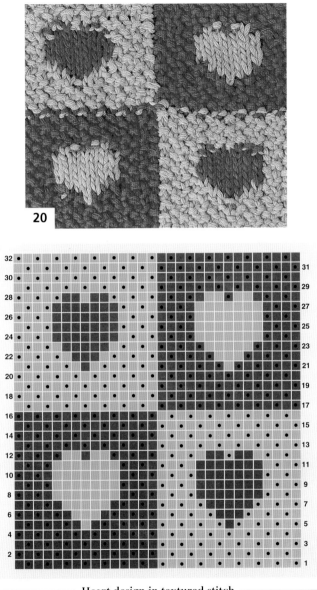

Heart design in textured stitch

DK linen, multiple of 30 stitches

The Stitch Collection

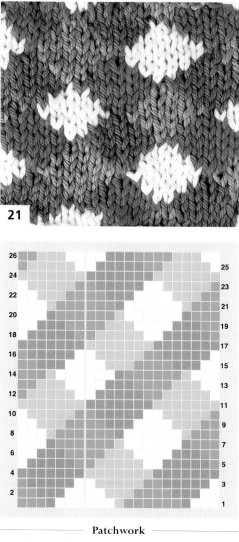

234

Patchwork

Medium-weight cotton, multiple of 14 stitches + 7

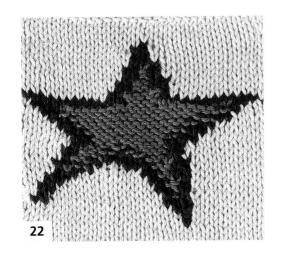

22

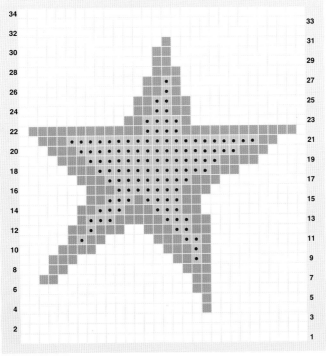

Star in a textured stitch

4-ply cotton, motif of 30 stitches

The Stitch Collection

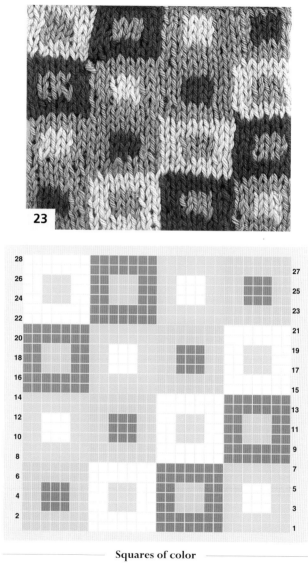

23

Squares of color

4-ply cotton, multiple of 28 stitches

The Stitch Collection

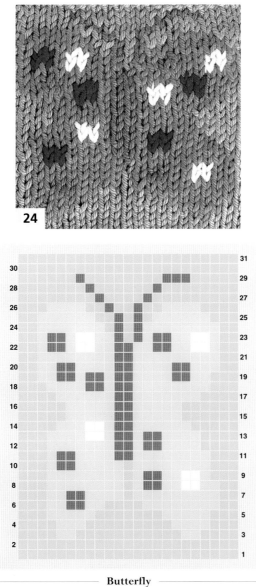

24

Butterfly

Medium-weight cotton, motif of 23 stitches

The Stitch Collection

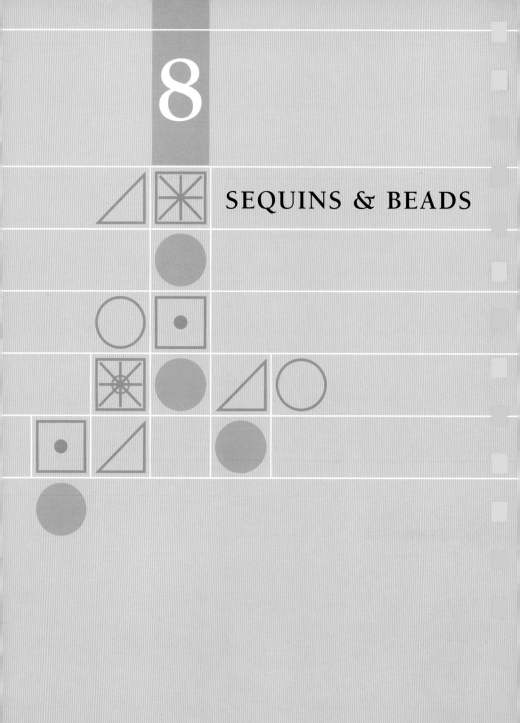

8

SEQUINS & BEADS

Working with sequins & beads

When working with beads and sequins, whether on a garment or a product, you need to begin by threading adequate numbers onto the ball of yarn.

- **To thread beads onto the yarn:**
  Use a fine sewing needle to thread the beads or sequins onto a piece of cotton or nylon thread. Then tie the end of the thread to the yarn, and slide the beads or sequins from the cotton down onto the yarn.

- **To place a bead on a right side knit row:**

  1 Bring the yarn to the front of the work (right side).
  2 Push the bead up to the top of the yarn.
  3 Slip the next stitch purlways from the left needle to right needle, and then take the yarn to the back of the work. This now leaves the bead sitting in the front of the slipped stitch.

- **To place a bead on the right side purl row:**
  Keep yarn at the front (right side) of the work and slip the bead up to the stitch just worked. Then slip the next stitch purlways from left needle to right needle, leaving the bead sitting in front of the slipped stitch. The bead will be secured when the next stitch is purled.

- **To place the bead on the right side when working wrong side purl row:**
  Take yarn to the back (right side) of the work, and slip the bead up to the stitch just worked. Slip next stitch purlways from left needle to right needle and bring yarn to front (wrong side) of the work, leaving the bead sitting in front of the slipped stitch on the right side of work.

- **When working with sequins:**
  Use sequins in the same way as beads, but ensure that they lie flat against the right side of the knitting.

1

240

Stocking stitch with diamond design in beads

4-ply cotton, multiple of 23 stitches + 6

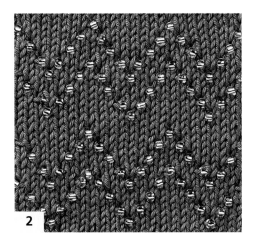

2

Stocking stitch with zigzag design in beads

Light-weight cotton, multiple of 8 stitches + 9

The Stitch Collection

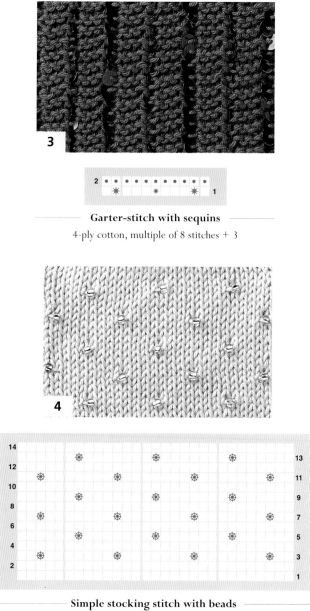

Garter-stitch with sequins

4-ply cotton, multiple of 8 stitches + 3

Simple stocking stitch with beads

4-ply cotton, multiple of 8 stitches + 5

The Stitch Collection

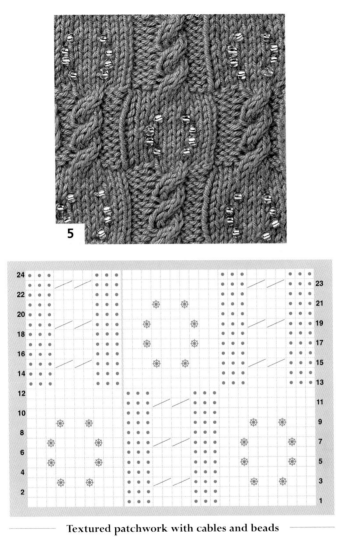

5

Textured patchwork with cables and beads

4-ply cotton, multiple of 20 stitches + 10

The Stitch Collection

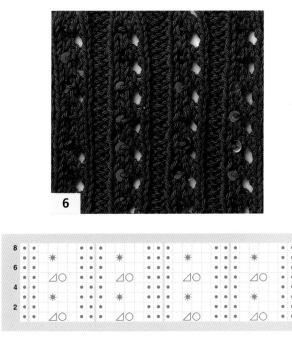

6

Lacy rib with sequins

4-ply cotton, multiple of 7 stitches + 1

7

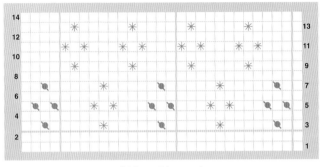

14									13
12									11
10									9
8									7
6									5
4									3
2									1

Bobbles with sequins

4-ply cotton, multiple of 12 stitches + 5

multiple of 12 rows + 2

8

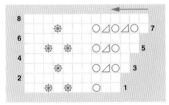

8							
6			❋		O△O△O		7
4		✺	✺		O△O		5
2		❋			O△O		3
		✺	✺		O		1

Lace edging with beads

DK wool cotton, multiple of 10 stitches, increasing to 13

The Stitch Collection

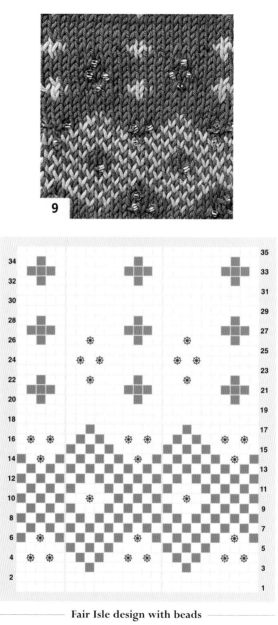

Fair Isle design with beads

Light-weight cotton, multiple of 10 stitches + 15

The Stitch Collection

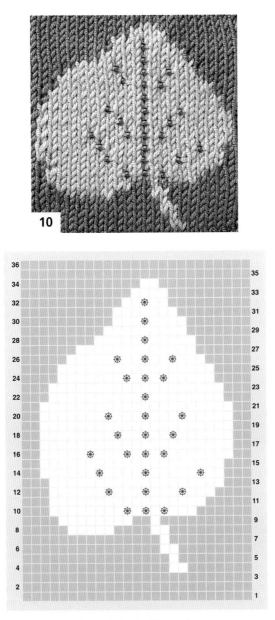

Intarsia leaf with beads

DK wool cotton, multiple of 25 stitches

The Stitch Collection

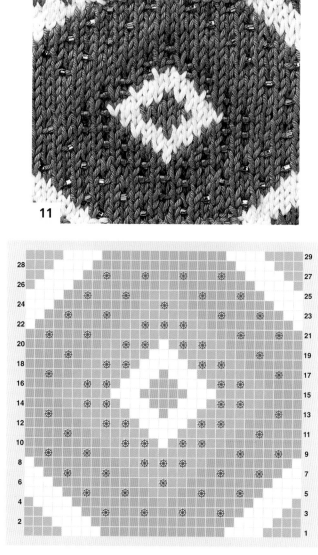

11

Intarsia diamond with beads

Light-weight cotton, multiple of 29 stitches

The Stitch Collection

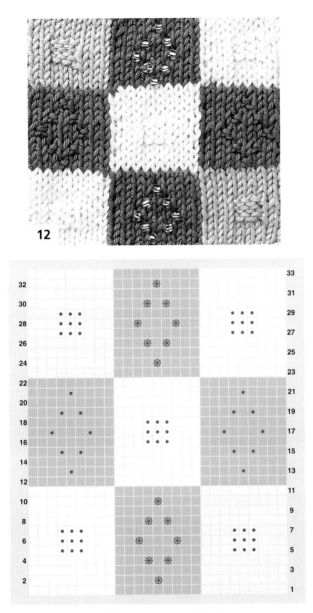

Intarsia textured patchwork with beaded diamonds
Light-weight cotton, multiple of 27 stitches

The Stitch Collection

Chart Symbols

Knit on RS rows, purl on WS rows.

Purl on RS rows, knit on WS rows.

Knit tbl on RS rows, purl tbl on WS rows.

Cast off the number of stitches indicated by the length of the arrow.

k2tog on RS rows, p2tog on WS rows.

p2tog on RS rows, k2tog on WS rows.

skpo on RS rows, p2tog tbl on WS rows.

p2tog tbl on RS rows, skpo on WS rows.

sl1, k2tog, psso on RS rows,
sl1, p2tog, psso on WS rows.

Central decrease. On RS (knit) rows, insert needle into next 2 stitches as if to knit them together but slip onto right-hand needle. k1, pass the two slipped stitches over together. On WS (purl) rows, slip 2 stitches knitwise and return to left-hand needle. Insert right-hand needle from back into second stitch then into first stitch, slip the 2 stitches from left-hand to right-hand needle, p1, and pass the 2 slipped stitches over.

k3tog on RS rows, p3tog on WS rows.

k3tog on RS rows, p3tog on WS rows.

p3tog on RS rows, k3tog on WS rows.

sl2 wyab, k3tog, p2sso on RS rows,
sl2 wyif, p3tog, p2sso on WS rows.

From the back of the work, bring the yarn over the needle to the front of the work, then between the needles to the back of the work again to make a stitch, k1, and pass the stitch previously slipped over both the yo and k1.

k4tog on RS rows, p4tog on WS rows.

p4tog on RS rows, k4tog on WS rows.

k5tog on RS rows, p5tog on WS rows.

p5tog on RS rows, k5tog on WS rows.

sl3, k1, pass the three slipped stitches over separately.

yo or yrn to make a stitch on RS rows or on WS rows.

Make 1 purlwise by purling tbl into the thread immediately between the stitch on the right-hand needle and the stitch on the left-hand needle on RS rows or on WS rows.

Knit into front and back of same stitch on RS rows or on WS rows.

Knit into front and back of same stitch on RS rows or on WS rows.

Purl into front and back of same stitch on RS rows or on WS rows.

(k1, p1, k1) all into same stitch on RS or on WS rows.

(k1, p1, k1) all into same stitch on RS or on WS rows.

(k1, yo, k1) all into same stitch on RS or on WS rows.

(k1, p1, k1, p1) all into same stitch on RS or on WS rows.

(k1, p1, k1, p1) all into same stitch on RS or on WS rows.

(k1, p1, k1, p1, k1) all into same stitch on RS or on WS rows.

(p1, yo, p1, yo, p1) all into same stitch on RS or on WS rows.

(k1, yo, k1) all into same stitch. Turn. p1, p1 tbl, k1. Turn. Knit into front and back of all 3 stitches. Do not turn. Pass all stitches one at a time over first stitch. Bobble completed.

(k1, yo, k1) all into same stitch. Turn. p3. Turn. k3. Turn. p3. Turn. sl1, k2tog, psso. Bobble completed.

(k1, p1, k1) all into same stitch. Pass all stitches one at a time over first stitch. Bobble completed.

(k1, p1, k1, p1, k1) all into same stitch. Pass all stitches one at a time over first stitch. Bobble completed.

(k1, yo, k1, yo, k1) all into same stitch. Turn. p5. Turn. k5. Turn. p5. Turn. p2tog, p1, p2tog. Turn. sl1, k2tog, psso. Bobble completed.

Insert needle into this stitch and the next stitch as if to k2tog but (k1, p1, k1, p1) into them. Turn. k1, p1, k1, p1. Turn. p1, k1, p1, k1. Turn. k1, p1, k1, p1. Turn. p2tog, p2tog tbl. Bobble completed.

⬤

(k1, p1, k1, p1, k1) all into same stitch. Turn. p5. Turn. Pass second, third, fourth, and fifth stitches over the first stitch one at a time then knit into back of this stitch. Bobble completed.

✳

Add bead.

✳

Add sequin. The size of the symbol will indicate larger or smaller sequins.

(k5, turn, p5, turn) 3 times on these 5 stitches.

🔲

k4, wrapping yarn twice around needle for each stitch on RS or on WS rows.

▢

k4, dropping the extra loops made on the previous row on RS or on WS rows.

∴

p3 from previous row on RS rows, k3 from previous row on WS rows.

▣

k3 from the stitches formed on RS rows, p3 from the stitches formed on WS rows.

•••••

p5 on RS rows, k5 on WS rows.

Slip 4 stitches onto cable needle. Wind yarn clockwise around base of cable needle 4 times, ending with yarn at back of work. Slip stitches onto right-hand needle and continue across row.

⬤ ⬤ ⬤

Bring yarn to front of work. Slip 9 stitches onto cable needle. Wind yarn clockwise around base of cable needle 4 times (i.e. around the 9 stitches on cable needle), ending with yarn at back of work. Slip stitches onto right-hand needle and continue across row.

Front cross. Knit second stitch on needle from behind the first stitch, knit first stitch on needle and slip both stitches off needle together.

Back cross. Knit second stitch on needle from in front of the first stitch, knit first stitch on needle and slip both stitches off the needle together.

╲╲

Slip 1 stitch onto cable needle and hold at front of work, k1, k1 from cable needle.

╳╳

Slip 1 stitch onto cable needle and hold at front of work, k1, k1 from cable needle.

╱╱

Slip 1 stitch onto cable needle and hold at back of work, k1, k1 from cable needle.

Chart Symbols

On RS and WS rows, slip 1 stitch onto cable needle and hold at back of work, k1, k1 from cable needle.

On RS and WS rows, slip 1 stitch onto cable needle and hold at front of work, p1, k1 from cable needle.

Slip 1 stitch onto cable needle and hold at back of work, k1, p1 from cable needle.

Slip 1 stitch onto cable needle and hold at front of work, p1, k1 from cable needle.

Slip 1 stitch onto cable needle and hold at back of work, k1, p1 from cable needle.

Slip 2 stitches onto cable needle and hold at front of work, k1, k2 from cable needle.

Slip 1 stitch onto cable needle and hold at back of work, k2, k1 from cable needle.

Slip 2 stitches onto cable needle and hold at front of work, p1, k2 from cable needle.

Slip 1 stitch onto cable needle and hold at back of work, k2, p1 from cable needle.

Slip 2 stitches onto cable needle and hold at back of work, k1, k2 from cable needle.

On RS rows slip 2 stitches onto cable needle and hold at front of work, k2, k2 from cable needle. On WS rows slip 2 stitches onto cable needle and hold at front of work, p2, p2 from cable needle.

Slip 2 stitches onto cable needle and hold at front of work, k2, k2 from cable needle.

On RS rows slip 2 stitches onto cable needle and hold at back of work, k2, k2 from cable needle. On WS rows slip 2 stitches onto cable needle and hold at back of work, p2, p2 from cable needle.

Slip 2 stitches onto cable needle and hold at back of work, k2, k2 from cable needle.

Slip 2 stitches onto cable needle and hold at front of work, p2, k2 from cable needle.

Slip 2 stitches onto cable needle and hold at back of work, k2, p2 from cable needle.

253

Slip 2 stitches onto cable needle and hold at front of work, p2, k2 from cable needle.

Slip 2 stitches onto cable needle and hold at back of work, k2, p2 from cable needle.

Slip 1 stitch onto cable needle and hold at back of work, k3, p1 from cable needle.

Slip 3 stitches onto cable needle and hold at front of work, p1, k3 from cable needle.

Slip 2 stitches onto cable needle and hold at front of work, p1, k1, (p1, k1) from cable needle.

Slip 1 stitch onto cable needle and hold at front of work, slip 3 stitches onto a second cable and hold at back of work, k1, k3 from second cable needle, k1 from first cable needle.

On RS rows, slip 3 stitches onto a cable needle and hold at back of work, k2, k3 from cable needle. On WS rows, slip 2 stitches onto cable needle and hold at back of work, p3, p2 from cable needle.

On RS rows, slip 2 stitches onto cable needle and hold at front of work, (k2, p1), k2 from cable needle. On WS rows, slip 3 stitches onto cable needle and hold at front of work, p2, (k1, p2) from cable needle.

On RS rows slip 3 stitches onto cable needle and hold at back of work, k2, (p1, k2) from cable needle. On WS rows, slip 2 stitches onto cable needle and hold at back of work, p2, k1, (p2) from cable needle.

On RS rows slip 3 stitches onto cable needle an hold at back of work, k2, (p1, k2) from cable needle. On WS rows, slip 2 stitches onto cable needle and hold at back of work, p2, k1 (p2) from cable needle.

Slip 3 stitches onto cable needle and hold at front of work, k3, k3 from cable needle.

Slip 3 stitches onto a cable needle and hold at back of work, k3, k3 from cable needle.

Slip 3 stitches onto a cable needle and hold at front of work, k3, k3 from cable needle.

Slip 3 stitches onto cable needle and hold at back of work, k3, k3 from cable needle.

Slip 3 stitches onto cable needle and hold at front of work, p3, k3 from cable needle.

Slip 3 stitches onto cable needle and hold at back of work, k3, p3 from cable needle.

Slip 1 stitch onto cable needle and hold at front of work, k5, k1 from cable needle.

Chart Symbols

Slip 5 stitches onto cable needle and hold at back of work, k1, k5 from cable needle.

Slip 1 stitch onto cable needle and hold at front of work, slip 2 stitches onto a second cable needle and hold at back of work, k2, k1 from first cable needle, k1, k2 from second cable needle.

Worked on a WS row. Slip 2 stitches onto cable needle and hold at back of work, slip 2 stitches onto a second cable needle and hold at front of work, p2, k2 from second cable needle and then p2 from first cable needle.

Worked on a WS row. Slip 2 stitches onto cable needle and hold at back of work, slip 4 stitches onto a second cable needle and hold at back of work, k2, p4 from second cable needle and then k2 from first cable needle.

Slip 4 stitches onto cable needle and hold at front of work, k4, k4 from cable needle.

Slip 4 stitches onto cable needle and hold at back of work, k4, k4 from cable needle.

On RS rows, slip 5 stitches onto cable needle and hold at back of work, k4, k5 from cable needle. On WS rows, slip 4 stitches onto cable needle and hold at back of work, p5, p4 from cable needle.

Slip 3 stitches onto cable needle and hold at back of work, slip 3 stitches onto a second cable needle and hold at front of work, k3, k3 from second cable needle, k3 from first cable needle.

Slip 5 stitches onto a cable needle and hold at front of work, k5, k5 from cable needle.

Slip 5 stitches onto a cable needle and hold at back of work, k5, k5 from cable needle.

sl1 purlwise with yarn at back.

sl1 with yarn at front.

Knit into the stitch of the row below on RS rows or WS rows.

■

No stitch.

⑤

(k1, yo, k1, yo, k1) all into 1 stitch making 5 stitches from one. Turn, k5. Turn, p5, lift fourth, third, second, and first stitches over fifth, and off the needle.

255

Chart Symbols

Abbreviations

back of work – the side of the knitted piece facing away from you as you are working across the row; do not confuse with WS
front of work – the side of the knitted piece facing as you are working across the row; do not confuse with RS
knitwise – inserting the needle into stitch as if to knit
purlwise – inserting the needle into stitch as if to purl

k	knit
k2tog	knit 2 stitches together
k2tog tbl	knit 2 stitches together through back of loops
k3tog	knit 3 stitches together
k4tog	knit 4 stitches together
k5tog	knit 5 stitches together
mb	make bobble; instructions will be given on how to make the bobble
m1	make 1 bobble by picking up the bar between the stitches on the right-hand and the left-hand needle, and knitting or purling into the back of it
p	purl
p2sso	pass 2 slipped stitches over
p2tog	purl 2 stitches together
p2tog tbl	purl 2 stitches together through back of loops
p3tog	purl 3 stitches together

p4tog	purl 4 stitches together
p5tog	purl 5 stitches together
psso	pass slipped stitch over, purlwise insert needle into the stitch as if to purl it
rep	repeat
RS	right side of knitted piece (the side that will be on show when worn or used)
skpo	slip one stitch, knit one stitch, pass slipped stitch over
sl	slip (the number of stitches stated). If knitwise or purlwise is not stated, stitches are usually slipped purlwise.
st	stitch
sts	stitches
tbl	through back of loops
tog	together
WS	wrong side of the knitted piece (the side that will not show when worn or used)
wyab	with yarn at back of the work
wyif	with yarn at front of the work
yb	yarn back; take yarn between needles from front to back of work
yf	yarn forward; bring yarn between needles from back to front of work; in older patterns, means the same as yo
yo	yarn over the needle to make a stitch; in some patterns yo is used to mean both yarn over and yarn around needle to make a stitch
yrn	yarn around needle; wrap yarn around needle to make a stitch